noborderland

noborderland

FINDING AMAZING GRACE IN A DARK AND DYING WORLD

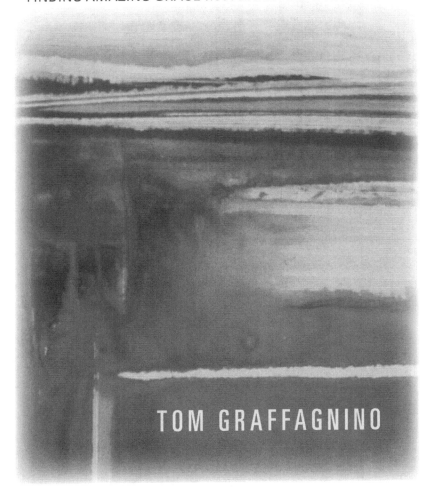

TOM GRAFFAGNINO

credo
house publishers

Published in the United States by Credo House Publishers,
a division of Credo Communications, LLC, Grand Rapids, Michigan
credohousepublishers.com

ISBN: 978-1-62586-157-3

Cover and interior design by Sharon VanLoozenoord
Editing by Donna Huisjen
Cover painting by Tom Graffagnino, 1981

Printed in the United States of America

First edition

CONTENTS

INTRODUCTION

As a new Christian in the mid 1990s, I was introduced to "Creed," a poem written in the 1970s by the British poet and journalist Steve Turner. The poem struck a spiritual nerve. Turner's insightful use of biting satire and irony helped clarify for me the stark contrast between the gospel-centered biblical message and all other religious worldviews and philosophies of man. Turner's "Creed" cut to the quick and penetrated deeply:

> We believe in Marxfreudanddarwin.
> We believe everything is OK
> as long as you don't hurt anyone,
> to the best of your definition of hurt,
> and to the best of your knowledge.
>
> We believe in sex before during
> and after marriage.
> We believe in the therapy of sin.
> We believe that adultery is fun.
> We believe that sodomy's OK
> We believe that taboos are taboo.
>
> ———
>
> We believe there's something in horoscopes,
> UFO's and bent spoons;
> Jesus was a good man just like Buddha
> Mohammed and ourselves.
> He was a good moral teacher although we think
> his good morals were bad.

We believe that all religions are basically the same,
at least the one that we read was.
They all believe in love and goodness.
They only differ on matters of
creation sin heaven hell God and salvation.

We believe that after death comes The Nothing
because when you ask the dead what happens
they say Nothing.
If death is not the end, if the dead have lied,
then it's compulsory heaven for all
excepting perhaps Hitler, Stalin and Genghis Khan.

————————

We believe that man is essentially good.
It's only his behaviour that lets him down.
This is the fault of society.
Society is the fault of conditions.
Conditions are the fault of society.

We believe that each man must find the truth
that is right for him.
Reality will adapt accordingly.
The universe will readjust. History will alter.
We believe that there is no absolute truth
excepting the truth that there is no absolute truth.

We believe in the rejection of creeds.

If Chance be the Father of all flesh,
disaster is His rainbow in the sky.
And when you hear "State of Emergency,"
"Sniper Kills Ten," "Troops on Rampage,"
"Youths Go Looting," "Bomb Blasts School,"
it is but the sound of man worshiping his maker.[1]

The conflict between the biblical worldview and all other world-view systems so poignantly laid bare by Turner is not imagined. The inconsistencies and illogical absurdities brought to light in "Creed" point to an underlying spiritual problem that cannot be solved or overcome by purely human effort or good intentions. The Bible teaches that fallen man's spiritual condition is dire and deadly and claims that the rebellion is as universal as it is personal.

Mankind's problem is sin, and all of creation is groaning under the weight of sin's deadly affliction.

We, as individuals, stand guilty before a holy God. There are no exceptions. There is no one righteous—no, not one (see Romans 3:10). We are idolaters through and through, whether we recognize the affliction or not. John Calvin once proclaimed, I think correctly, that "the human mind is a perpetual forge of idols."

We need a Savior.

Quite naturally, the world dismisses the true message of the Bible. To the cultural elite, there is no crisis, no spiritual "war," no deadly snare at all. To the unregenerate man, the saving gospel message of the cross is simply foolishness (1 Corinthians 1:18), an embellished tall tale devised by men and really nothing more.

At best, the juggernaut of contemporary secular progressivism imagines the Bible to be an outdated compilation of do's and don'ts, therapeutic metaphors, and allegories written long ago to help the gullible and simple-minded to achieve a fleeting degree of inner peace and self-satisfaction. Indeed, the more progressively "enlightened" among us today insist that the Bible may be a helpful resource for the unsophisticated and the insecure, but that it certainly is *not* the direct, verbally transmitted Word of God and surely *not* the key to eternal life in glory. In some cases, we are told by the secular humanists that the Scriptures may be psychologically beneficial for some, but really nothing more. After all, the world's experts, steeped in naturalism's concocted brews, inform us that we are all basically good and that we can live purposeful and successful lives if and when we learn to "give peace a chance." By employing the techniques that progressive humanism has to offer, we can overcome.

The implication that mankind is truly fallen and in desperate need of a Savior, as the Scriptures clearly teach, is simply unacceptable to the secular mind. To the sensibilities of proud, postmodern man, to suggest that "the heart is deceitful above all things and beyond cure" (Jeremiah 17:9) is itself a desperately wicked, even blasphemous notion to entertain. For most today, insisting that we are unrighteous "sinners," justly condemned before a Holy God, has practically become the unforgiveable sin.

In the educated opinion of the vast majority of secular humanists, and in the eyes of a large segment of theological liberals, Jesus, if he actually existed at all, is simply reduced to a (mostly) positive influence. He may be venerated as an admirable teacher and a good neighbor . . . "just like Buddha, Mohammed, and ourselves." He is generally presented as a well-intentioned, gentle sort with an always captivating, benevolent smile . . . a misunderstood community organizer and social justice warrior who met a sadly tragic end.

After all, we are told, didn't Jesus come to help us achieve deep inner peace? Didn't He come to offer us good advice and better social skills to help usher in a New Age of healthy self-esteem and utopian contentment here and now?

Well, no. Not really.

Turner's "Creed" calls attention to the fact that the human spiritual condition is anything but pretty and that the Good News of the gospel is anything but easy to swallow. Turner's poem cuts through all the philosophical and therapeutic niceties that are so often passed along as the gospel truth. The poem underscores the deception that has so successfully blinded the hearts and minds of men. Bluntly stated, the problem with the world is sin. The world is locked in proud, idolatrous rebellion. "Creed" drives home the point.

Jesus was much more than the Nice Guy from Galilee with innovative, helpful hints for righteous living. Jesus stilled the stormy Sea of Galilee at one point with a word, but He made life-threatening, tsunami-like spiritual waves everywhere else. He came to rock humanity's boat. He did so two thousand years ago, and He still does so today. "Do not suppose that I have come to bring peace to the earth. I did not come to bring peace, but a sword. For I have come to turn "'a man against his father, a daughter against her mother, a daughter-in-law against her mother-in-law—a man's enemies will be the members of his own household'"" (Matthew 10:34–36).

These are not exactly words of an itinerant flower child or a kindly Jewish philosopher making the rounds through the countryside of ancient Israel. While I am sure that we would like to tip-toe past these disturbing "red letter" words of the Messiah, I am persuaded that we do so ill-advisedly and at our own eternal peril. We may first encounter baby Jesus, "meek and mild" in the manger, but that is not where He would leave us.

Obviously, the "All You Need Is Love" Jesus is very popular today. That Jesus fits the mold that the world cherishes and approves. After all, *that* Jesus meets all of the requirements, expectations, and sentimental aspirations of the world. This Jesus Much-Preferred is always agreeable, always friendly, "progressive," and fashionably up-to-date. He is the Convenient Jesus whom even the most hardened, confirmed atheist might grow to tolerate and even admire.

But the Jesus of the Bible, the Jesus of Matthew 10:34–36 and elsewhere, is much more dangerous than that. He is not simply a Servant-Lamb who aims to please. He is also the Prophet-King and the roaring Lion. He is Lord of lords. He is "Holy, Holy, Holy," alive and well and coming again to judge the quick and the dead. We dare not forget this straightforward scriptural truth. Today, however, many have chosen to do just that. Preaching a half-baked, sugar-coated message to enthusiastic, smiling crowds has become, too often, standard fare.

I am convinced that much of the professing church today in the Western world has been lulled to sleep by the well-intentioned philosophies of learned men, New Age accredited spiritual systems, and all the "latest things." We have been swamped by the lukewarm waters of compromise and mesmerizing higher critical doubt. We have been enticed by Hollywood glitter. We long to be caressed and entertained by time-bound pleasantries, not confronted by difficult, life-giving, and life-preserving eternal truth. We have too often substituted the Word of God with self-aggrandizing, feel-good platitudes. We expect our under-shepherds in the pulpit to coddle us with easygoing tales and social justice flatteries. We gladly surround ourselves with comforting conveniences of every sort. We are distracted by legions of golden calf addictions. We demand soothing half-truths and innocuous "have-it-your-way" relativisms that stupefy the mind and eventually sear the conscience.

For the most part, we have abandoned the teaching and preaching that bring sinners to their knees. We are no longer sinners in the hands of an angry God. We are, instead, temporarily wayward patients in psychoanalytic therapy. Francis Schaeffer has expressed it well: "Few believe in guilt anymore. There is only 'sickness,' or 'guilt feelings,' or 'sociological non-conformity.' There is no such thing as true [moral] guilt."[2]

Richard John Neuhaus put it this way: "The dismal reality is that the church's native language of sin and grace, right and wrong, truth and falsehood, is in danger of being displaced by the vocabulary of psychology, law and public relations."[3]

We have tiptoed past the convicting, prophetic voice of Scripture that boldly declares us "Guilty!" In doing so, we foolishly think that we are doing ourselves a favor. Thinking ourselves wise (sensitive, caring, and fair), we have become fools. For convenience's sake, we have melted down the penetrating, razor sharp, double-edged sword of truth and fashioned for ourselves psychological, snub-nosed butter knives instead. We have redefined "tolerance" to mean benign neutrality and/or unquestioned acceptance so that no one is offended. Tolerance reigns supreme.

I have written this book from a Bible-believing perspective. I believe that the Bible is God-breathed and inerrant. I am persuaded that the Word became flesh and dwelt among us to bring hope to a dying, sinful world. I believe that this true and Living Hope does not come to us on a bed of sweet-smelling roses or as a reward for our good works, sincerity, or well-intentioned efforts. This hope is not brought to us via the countless therapeutic mental exercises and paths toward transcendent inner peace and greater self-esteem, but by revelation—and this from the sovereign, amazing grace of God through the strait gate of mournful repentance and faith in Jesus, the resurrected Lord.

I am convinced that eternal life in glory comes only when sinners are first confronted with the hard truth of our fallen, sinful condition as revealed by the Holy Spirit through hearing God's Holy Word. When we are made aware of our guilt before God, we see ourselves as desperately "poor in spirit" and find ourselves swinging helplessly at the end of our spiritual rope; then and only then may we be truly blessed, rescued, and born again. This is a divine act of grace from beginning to end, according to the plan and purpose of a merciful God.

"Progressive" Christendom today has crafted its own variety of world-pleasing and self-serving messages. The apostle Paul would have recognized these fashionably apostate and sometimes heretical messages for what they are. He had some very harsh words for those who would proclaim a "different," perverted gospel: "Evidently some people are throwing you into confusion and are trying to pervert the gospel of Christ. But even if we or an angel from heaven should preach a gospel other than the one we preached to you, let them be under God's curse!" (Galatians 1:7b–8).

New and improved philosophies and scientific advancements cannot and will not save the world. Quick-fix solutions sponsored by the brightest minds promoting the "latest thing" are doomed always to eventual failure. The idols of religious humanism have changed very little over time. They come today in shinier packages with "smarter," more sophisticated parts. They come with more enticing bells and whistles, and with high resolution graphics, but in the end they are only worn-out variations of the golden calf first fashioned at the foot of Mt. Sinai 3,500 years ago. The idols always fall short. They are impotent accessories, designed to appease the vanities, and are destined only to melt down. Nevertheless, with eyes closed tightly and fingers crossed, we proudly continue adding bricks to the latest Babel tower, hoping against hope that "next time," on that next step higher up, we'll make *the discovery* that changes everything. We will concoct better gods of our own choosing, gods that promise to add true meaning to our lives and save us from meaninglessness and ultimate destruction.

And so, the idols, our "other gods," continue to entice. They are proudly presented to us clothed in sequined, intellectual vestments. Their names and pleasure-promising appearances are legion. Their appeal is subtle and always tempting. They are introduced under the guise of nuanced sophistication, enlightened jargon, and always with mesmerizing charm. The perpetually repackaged message ("Did God *really* say . . . ?") never relents. Satan, our postmodern foundation dismantler, continues his work of confusion and destruction with his honey-dipped propositional half-truths. And his flaming arrows continue to fly.

This book is a compilation of observations, opinions, and poems. The poems often ride piggy-back on the thoughts of noted Christian apologists, theologians, philosophers, scientists, and cultural commentators.

My use of satire, irony, parody, and hyperbole may cause some to recoil a bit, I am sure. There are many today who are convinced that the Christian message of the Bible should never make waves or cause discomfort.

My understanding is that the word *satire* ultimately is derived from Latin words meaning "fed up." When the prophets, the apostles, and Jesus himself were fed up with the destructive folly and idolatrous notions of men and with the wayward apostasies of their contemporary religious leaders, they sometimes confronted them with the skewering rebuke of penetrating satire. As the author and conservative evangelical pastor Douglas Wilson puts it, "Nothing is more serious than the sin of idolatry, but this did not keep the prophets from making fun of it."[4]

It seems that some have been conditioned to believe that the gospel of Jesus Christ must always be more about being "nice" than about being truthful. Compromised, watered down preaching and teaching over several generations have had disastrous moral and existential consequences for Western civilization. Those consequences have been bleeding out into every corner of the contemporary public square. Every aspect of our culture has been affected. No one is untouched. And nothing is sacred.

In 1983, Alexandr Solzhenitsyn recognized the danger. He saw the writing on the wall when he declared:

> As a survivor of the Communist Holocaust I am horrified to witness how my beloved America, my adopted country, is gradually being transformed into a secularist and atheistic utopia, where communist ideals are glorified and promoted, while Judeo-Christian values and morality are ridiculed and increasingly eradicated from the public and social consciousness of our nation. Under the decades-long assault and militant radicalism of many so-called "liberal" and "progressive" elites, God has been progressively erased from our public and educational institutions, to be replaced with all manner of delusion, perversion, corruption, violence, decadence, and insanity.[5]

One would have to be willfully blind not to notice the lawless slide into decadence and immorality today in the West. The prophets in the Old Testament, the apostles in the New Testament, and Jesus in the Gospels recognized and addressed the same drift in their days. I am persuaded that today, *especially* today, we are in need of pointed, persistent, prophetic warning more so than ever before.

Almost three thousand years ago, Hosea, God's prophet to the idolatrous and apostate nation of Israel, saw the same writing on the wall that we can see today. Those who are familiar with the Old Testament Scriptures are familiar with the prophet's assessment:

"They sow the wind and reap the whirlwind. The stalk has no head; it will produce no flour. Were it to yield grain, foreigners would swallow it up" (Hosea 8:7).

Much of the professing church in the Western world, in an effort to be culturally "relevant," has too often offered headless stalks of grain. The compromised and compromising contemporary church has sown the wind. Now there is a spiritual famine in the land. The walls of conservative Christian orthodoxy have been purposefully deconstructed and breached. Under the acid reign of political correctness and blind "tolerance," the ancient guardrails of truth and reason have dissolved, moral foundations have been undermined, and sacred fences have been removed. There is trouble in *No Border Land*.

Carl F. Henry, echoing Solzhenitsyn's prophetic appraisal, stated:

> A half-generation ago the pagans were still largely threatening at the gates of Western culture; now the barbarians are plunging into the . . . mainstream. As they seek to reverse the inherited intellectual and moral heritage of the Bible, . . . [we are] engaged as never before in a rival conflict for the mind, the conscience, the will, the spirit, the very selfhood of contemporary man.[6]

No Border Land is written with three purposes. First, it is intended to be prophetic in nature, a warning as well as a lament. Secondly, it is an appeal to the fence-straddling, contemporary Laodicean church to rouse herself, repair the wall, and heed the Shepherd's voice. Finally, it is a gospel apologetic, a call to consider and respond to the biblical message of the cross.

In the words of J. I. Packer,

> The apologetic strategy that would attract converts by the flattery of accommodating the gospel to the "wisdom" of sinful man was condemned by Paul nineteen centuries ago, and the past hundred years have provided a fresh demonstration of its bankruptcy. The world may call its compromises "progressive" and "enlightened" (those are its names for all forms of thought that pander to its conceit); those who produce them will doubtless, by a natural piece of wishful thinking, call them "bold" and "courageous," and perhaps "realistic" and "wholesome," but the Bible condemns them as sterile aberrations. And the Church cannot hope to recover its power till it resolves to turn its back on them.[7]

Sinking in These Human Isms

"Don't let anyone capture you

with empty philosophies

and high-sounding nonsense

that come from human thinking

and from the spiritual powers

of this world, rather than from Christ."

(Colossians 2:8 NLT)

STIR THAT NEW, OLD PAGAN BREW

The persistent drumbeat of regressive paganism has been resounding through the past several generations of Western culture. The philosophical precepts of the new paganism have infiltrated every aspect of the modern world today. Her champions are many. Their names are well known, and their influence has been profound. They have been the movers and the shakers of humanism's juggernaut of change. Each one has made his or her unique contribution to the steady erosion of Western civilization's foundational beliefs. The pounding waves of philosophical naturalism, reductionism, and materialism have been relentless. Gradually, the religion of the imperial, autonomous Self has emerged and now reigns supreme.

Today, many of our Western cultural elite, steeped and immersed as they are in the philosophical cauldron of progressive academia, are blindly *regressing* into the dark fog of ancient paganism, all the while proudly calling the regression "positive change."

Pied Pipers of Idol Progress . . . at it again.

———

Double, double toil and trouble;
Fire burn and caldron bubble . . .[1]

———

Singer, Sanger, Kinsey, Leary,
Joseph Campbell, Jung and Freud . . .
Prophets of New Paganism,
Heroes of the coming Void.

Marx 'n' Nietzsche, Kundalini,
Foucault-Fun for Me and You!
Listen! . . . Sweat Lodge Kali-calling,
Stir that New, Old Pagan Brew.

Dawkins, Hawking: "God is nowhere!"
Pilate, Mephistopheles,
Merlin, Oprah, "What's your pleasure?"
Endless stream idolatries.

Rainbow-chasing Me, Me-isms,
No one even thinks it odd!
Nature-bending man "progressing". . .
(Taste the fruit and "Be like God!")

Narcissistic Selfie-Streaming
Campfire drumming, . . . Hollywood.
Lights-out, proudly Roe v. Wading
Back to Screwtape's neighborhood.

Welcome to the heart of darkness,
Stand with us on sinking sand.
Place your bets on "good intentions."
Welcome to No Border Land.

———————

Lord, forgive us! . . . Lord, have mercy!
Give us grace to see The Sin . . .
Help us hear the words of Jesus . . .
Lord, redeem us! . . . Come again!

The new paganism is the virtual divinization of man, the religion of man as the new God. One of its popular slogans, repeated often by Christians, is "the infinite value of the human person." Its aim is building a heaven on earth, a secular salvation. Another word for the new paganism is humanism, the religion that will not lift up its head to the heavens but stuffs the heavens into its head.[2] —PETER KREEFT

CHILDREN OF CHAOS

We are children of chaos, and the deep structure of change is decay. At root, there is only corruption, and the unstemmable tide of chaos. Gone is purpose; all that is left is direction. This is the bleakness we have to accept as we peer deeply and dispassionately into the heart of the Universe.[1] —PETER ATKINS

———

It's the bottom line we're facing . . .
And if Peter's really right . . .
There's direction but no purpose.
Mankind's Existential Blight.

And so, dwelling here in darkness,
There's no reason to complain . . .
Teaching children Hope is madness,
Madness now considered sane.

Daily headlines now confirm it . . .
Will to Power has her way.
It's the tar pit mankind fell for . . .
Chaos calls us to decay.

ALL OUR SACRED HUMAN ISMS

Someone once said that "when men stop believing in God, it is not that they believe in nothing; they will believe in anything."[1]

Humanism, the worldview that attempts to pull humanity up by its own bootstraps and then to set it finally straight, is discovering that in order to do so it must first pull the rug out from under its own presuppositions. If one's metaphysical starting point is "In the beginning, purposeless nature . . . ," the fabric of reason and meaning itself will over time quite naturally unravel. Reason will dismantle itself. It will deconstruct. Like the mythical serpent Ouroboros, it will devour itself in mad, gnostic fits of self-contradiction. Today those contradictions are becoming spectacularly apparent.

The Christian philosopher and author Phillip Johnson cut to the chase when he asked:

> Is God the true creator of everything that exists, or is God a product of the human imagination, real only in the minds of those who believe? . . . If God really does exist, then to lead a rational life a person has to take account of God and his purposes. A person or a society that ignores the Creator is ignoring the most important part of reality, and to ignore reality is to be irrational.[2]

The towering edifice of humanism will eventually collapse under the weight of its own intrinsic irrationalities. It is built, after all, on the sinking sand of subjective, autonomous pride. It is an idolatrous trap—a temptation of the first magnitude. The isms of idolatry have galloped into town on the back of many steeds: relativism, materialism, progressivism, secularism, scientism, postmodernism, nihilism, and more. The thundering hooves of this advancing philosophical horde can be detected everywhere today. The siege ramps of hubris and toxic incoherence are in place.

———————

Our most fundamental -Ism
Says "There's nothing absolute!"
That's the Ism we're most proud of . . .
One that no one may dispute!

But we've got some other Isms—
We've got plenty, sir, to spare.
Isms guaranteed to please you . . .
And to make things really fair.

All our fundamental-Isms
Are progressively inclined.
Some of those that we've come up with
Have been recently divined!

All of them are well-imagined
Each one sacrosanct-ified.
They're the Isms we're advancing
And from each and every side.

Now with all our human Isms
Not a thing can hold us back!
Yes, these fundamental-Isms
Make us leaders of the pack!

It's the way we're moving forward!
No more ball and no more chain!
Self-fulfillment beckons to us . . .
Now Subjectivism reigns.

Yes, our fundamental-Isms
Start and end with You and Me.
Long live Deconstruction-Isms
Built on Proud Autonomy!

DR. DUMPTY'S MASS DYSFUNCTION

In 1984, during a joint presentation with her husband Russell Kirk, Annette Kirk observed:

> What happens to language when words lose all significance, when they have no history or objectivity, when they are deconstructed or denied a reality? This is what has happened in recent years in the departments of literature and philosophy in leading universities. Is it any wonder that there is a crisis in the teaching of moral education, if words, which are the tools to convey truths, have no objective meaning?[1]

If Mrs. Russell Kirk thought things were spinning out of control in 1984, I can't imagine what she thinks today. Lewis Carroll makes much the same point:

> "When I use a word," Humpty Dumpty said, in rather a scornful tone, "it means just what I choose it to mean—neither more nor less."
>
> "The question is," said Alice, "whether you can make words mean so many different things."
>
> "The question is," said Humpty Dumpty, "which is to be master—that's all."[2]

Kids, when Humpty has the last word,
Sitting proudly on that wall . . .
Please take note and listen closely.
You'll detect the devil's call.

He's a "Good Egg" . . . Quite postmodern!
And he fits in well today.
Pay attention . . . He's got tenure!
(And he thinks of you as prey.)

Watch him deconstruct tradition,
Watch him undermine what's true.
Watch him re-imagine meaning . . .
Watch him pass it on to you.

Watch him feint with fancy footwork,
Watch the contradictions fly!
Watch him smugly laugh and chortle,
Watch the fog intensify.

Watch the crack-up of the culture,
As it's yoked to Satan's plan, . . .
Doctor Dumpty's mass dysfunction
Finds acceptance in the land.

Watch the chaos he's espousing,
Taking root around you, son . . .
Watch dysfunction celebrated
When ol' Humpty's said and done!

COME JABBERWOCK WITH ME AWHILE

In his book *The Atheist's Guide to Reality,* Dr. Alex Rosenberg, philosophy department chair at Duke University, boldly states that "we need to face the fact that nihilism is true."[1] He follows up with the astute observation that "the meanings we think are carried by our thoughts, our words, and our actions are just sand castles we build in the air."[2]

Think about that. Let it sink in.

Also, according to Dr. Rosenberg, "Science provides all the significant truths about reality. . . . Being scientistic just means treating science as our exclusive guide to reality, to nature—both our own nature and everything else's."[3] Apparently, when you're wandering through the tall weeds of proud delusion, reality can be difficult to ascertain. When nihilistic materialism reigns, and when religious scientism becomes one's go-to idol, irrationality will eventually bubble up to the surface and by default become one's standard of comprehension.

The Jabberwocky, perhaps, explains it best in Lewis Carroll's *Through the Looking-Glass:*

> Twas bryllyg, and ye slythy toves
> Did gyre and gymble in ye wabe:
> All mimsy were ye borogoves;
> And ye mome raths outgrabe. . . .
>
> "Beware the Jabberwock, my son!
> The jaws that bite, the claws that catch!
> Beware the Jubjubbird, and shun
> The fruminous Bandersnatch!"

He took the vorpal sword[4] in hand:
Long time the maxnome foe he sought—
So rested he by the Tum-tum tree,
And stood awhile in thought.

And, as in uffish thought he stood,
The Jabberwock, with eyes of flame,
Came whiffling through the tulgey wood,
And burbled as it came! . . .[5]

So, here we are . . . Western civilization, early twenty-first century. Welcome to Wonderland where, according to some, in the final analysis nothing is really real and everything is meaningless. We are witnessing today the incipient and incremental triumph of Jabberwocky-ism, where nonsense is hailed as deep thinking and utter foolishness touted as urbane wisdom.

When the very concept of spirit/mind is rejected, the default category is nihilistic nonsense—dangerous, destructive, delusional, nihilistic nonsense. When God (who is Spirit) is declared unwelcome and is dismissed by large segments of society, eventually the intelligentsia of materialism and secularism will feel free to seize control of the cultural reins.

And so, not unexpectedly and quite predictably, they are doing just that.

When I read Dr. Rosenberg's expanded version about how human beings come to understand things—"Thinking about things can't happen at all. . . . When consciousness convinces you that you, or your mind, or your brain has thoughts about things, it is wrong"[6]—my jaw dropped. I gasped in disbelief at the sheer irrationality of his truth-denouncing proclamation. But then I thought to myself . . . *Well, . . . perhaps, somewhere in a dark corner of Alice's Wonderland, there is a University of Jabberwocky that offers PhDs in Advanced Theoretical Nonsense, where the reality of truth and the truth of reality are denied . . . a place where deception is honored and the blind learn to lead the blind.*

Sadly, I'm afraid, this is the kind of thinking that more and more people in the upper echelons of the intellectual community seem to be enamored with. It seems that the mark of excellence—the "red badge of courage," if you will—for the postmodern deconstructionists in our midst is the ability to think illogical, self-refuting thoughts and then to proudly write a book about having them. Apparently, irrationality sells quite well in this so-called "enlightened" era, an age in which science has become a most imposing idol and a willing handmaiden to the golden calf of the Autonomous Self.

Revelation be damned.

———

Come Jabberwock with me awhile,
I'll teach you all you need!
You'll come away in dark dismay . . .
But wiser, son, indeed!

Just come along and listen now,
To my enlightened dream . . .
Let's have a talk . . . Let's Jabberwock.
You'll know just what I mean.

I'll take you straight into the night,
Where nothing's really real . . .
Please don't delay . . . I know the Way.
I think . . . therefore I *feel!*

Come "whiffle through my tulgey wood,"[5]
Where Science rules and reigns.
And there we'll greet new friends of meat
In nihilistic chains.

———————

Lord, give us Grace to see beyond
This darkness pressing in.
Please guide us then to see your Truth,
Enlightenment begin.

Lord, help us test the spirits now
That wish to kill and maim,
When Men of Meat bow at the feet
Of idols so inane.

And when we hide from Truth, dear Lord,
And claim all meaning's lost,
Please help us see on bended knee,
The meaning of the Cross.

———————

"I am the LORD,
  the Maker of all things,
  who stretches out the heavens,
  who spreads out the earth by myself,
who foils the signs of false prophets
  and makes fools of diviners,
who overthrows the learning of the wise
  and turns it into nonsense." (ISAIAH 44:24–25)

———

"There were some ages in Western history that have occasionally been called Dark. They were dark, it is said, because in them learning declined, and progress paused, and men labored under the pall of belief. A cause-effect relationship is frequently felt to exist between the pause and the belief. Men believed in things like the Last Judgment and fiery torment. . . . Then the light came. . . . Men were freed from the fear of the Last Judgment; it was felt to be more bracing to face Nothing than to face the Tribunal. . . . The myth sovereign in the old age was that everything means everything. The myth sovereign in the new is that nothing means anything.[7] —THOMAS HOWARD

IN THE MEANTIME, LET US PREY

Donna Gunderson Hailson notes that

> More than a century ago, Friedrich Nietzsche sug-
> gested that the idea of God was dead and, that if the
> world were to be without this sense of divine order
> and attaching moral principles, it would be left with
> nihilism—no meaning, no purpose, no intrinsic value.
> Nietzsche attributed two central principles of West-
> ern civilization to Christianity: all people are created
> equal and human life is precious. It is because we are
> created equal and in the image of God that our lives
> have moral worth and that we share the rights to life,
> liberty and the pursuit of happiness. Nietzsche's warn-
> ing was that none of these values would make sense
> without the background moral framework against
> which they were formulated. A post-Christian West, he
> argued, would have to go back to the ethical drawing
> board for a reconsideration of its values.[1]

At the drawing board of Nietzsche,
We've now gathered all around.
Prophets of mass de-construction
Madly seeking solid ground.

Truth's been taken off the table,
Ancient bound'ries? . . . All erased.
Moral principles? . . . Dismantled.
Sacred Virtues? . . . Now debased.

Indeed, Nietzsche saw it coming,
Darwin's fittest made it right.
Western culture's been rejected.
Mighty Self's our guiding light.

Subjectivity's the hammer . . .
Firm foundations chipped away.
Values now come by consensus.
In the meantime, let us prey.

1984

In his novel *1984* (written in 1949), George Orwell envisioned a time and place where a philosophical elite would be able to dictate reality according to their own vain and power-obsessed imaginings. At least a generation before terms like "deconstructionism," "postmodernism, "and "political correctness" began appearing on the scene, Orwell penned these prophetic words of a dystopian future in a totalitarian state, where certain thoughts would be outlawed and common sense would not be tolerated:

> In the end the Party would announce that two and two made five, and you would have to believe it. It was inevitable that they should make that claim sooner or later: the logic of their position demanded it. Not merely the validity of experience, but the very existence of external reality, was tacitly denied by their philosophy. The heresy of heresies was common sense. And what was terrifying was not that they would kill you for thinking otherwise, but that they might be right. For, after all, how do we know that two and two make four? Or that the force of gravity works? Or that the past is unchangeable? If both the past and the external world exist only in the mind, and if the mind itself is controllable— what then?[1]

Today, it seems, we have begun testing the dark and dangerous waters of Orwell's dystopian state and society. Tragically, many are calling it "progress."

———

Welcome to the barrel's bottom
Where the Light is less than dim.
Where the Truth's been deconstructed . . .
It's the mess we all stepped in.

Welcome to the Wake of Woodstock,
Roe with us into the night.
Wade with us into the quagmire.
Where what YOU decide is "right."

Jump right in the current fashion . . .
Welcome to the undertow.
Welcome to the Pilate Error.
Welcome to the wind we sow.

Welcome to the consequences
Of a nation gone astray.
Sixty million babies later,
We've become the devil's prey.

Look around! I think you'll like it!
Taste postmodernism's fruit.
Be your own Law, Judge, and Jury.
Humanism's absolute.

Tiptoe with me past this mirror
Just pretend you're well and "good."
It's not difficult to do, sir,
When there's no real Ought or Should.

His truth . . . her truth . . . that's the ticket!
My truth, your truth . . . cauldron stirred.
Our truth, their truth . . . insurrection.
(Never mind God's Truth . . .the Word.)

TOLERANCE NOW MEANS ACCEPTANCE

Tolerance now means "acceptance" . . .
We're all in with what you choose.
We agree now all is normal,
We don't do "Don'ts!" . . . Only "Do's."

That's the way we prove we're loving.
That's our only High Command.
That's the way we're making progress.
There's no line drawn in our sand.

Now we're sure you're in agreement,
But if not, we'd like to say . . .
"Just get lost" and . . . "Sayonara!"
"Adios! Just go away!"

"Hit the road! Your thought's offensive!"
"Your 'Good News' is just the pits . . ."
"Man, don't come around here preaching . . ."
"Our Big Brother says to quit."

THANK YOU SO MUCH, PETER PAN

Late in his life, *Playboy* magazine founder Hugh Hefner (b. 1926–d. 2017), made this illuminating claim: "Much of my life has been like an adolescent dream of an adult life. If you were still a boy, in almost a Peter Pan kind of way, and could have just the perfect life that you wanted to have, that's the life I invented for myself."[1]

The Playboy philosophy took root in the 1960s with a vengeance. It "flowered" at Woodstock in upstate New York at the end of the decade, where it teamed up with the smoke and mirrors of pharmacological vanities and an enflamed spirit of rebellious passion. Today we are stuck in the permanent purple haze of an adolescent Never Never Land, addicted to the bipolar dream of having it "Our Way" and feeling fine. The Lost Boys (and Girls) of Hefner's Never-Land have evolved into today's power brokers, and we are paying a very heavy price.

Social and political commentator Malcolm Muggeridge, before his death in 1990, observed: "If God is dead, somebody is going to have to take his place. It will be megalomania or erotomania, the drive for power or the drive for pleasure, the clenched fist or the phallus, Hitler or Hugh Hefner."[2]

Muggeridge did not foresee that the two dystopian "drives" would actually merge into one very ugly Western cultural train wreck.

———

Thank you so much, Mr. Playboy,
For the things you left behind,
For the fashion . . . and the passion (!)
Of the hedonistic mind.

Thank you for the Narcissism . . .
For the flesh we hold so dear!
For The Self-ish Code of Ethics,
And your lifestyle so sincere!

Thank you for that Me-First Vision
(Sir, you helped to set us free!).
Thank you for the death of marriage
And the end of decency.

Thank you for Pandora's Box, sir . . .
You so proudly opened wide.
Thank you for the slope so slipp'ry,
And the dark, descending slide.

Thank you for the paganism,
That today we find so "cool."
It's the gift that keeps on giving . . .
It's our Common Core in school!

Thank you for progressive thinking,
Thank you so much, Peter Pan . . .
Front and center . . . still unfolding
Here in Never-NeverLand.

Thank you for the adolescence
That is permanent today.
Thank you for all those abortions . . .
Thanks for helping pave the way!

Thank you for the family break-up!
Normalized pornography . . .
Thank you for the degradation . . .
Thank you for the poverty!

———————

Thank you for these contributions . . .
Hef, you helped us see the light!
Thank you for the Self-Indulgence
And promotion of this blight.

Thank you for the exploitation
And your twisted point of view.
Thank you, sir, from all the Lost Boys . . .
And now from the Lost Girls, too.

———————

"If a society is to preserve its stability and a degree of
continuity, it must know how to keep its adolescents
from imposing their tastes, attitudes, values, and fantasies on everyday life."[3] —ERIC HOFFER

Yes, the heart of man is wicked . . .
Lord, have mercy on us all.

ROE WITH US INTO THE QUAGMIRE

"Truth is no longer absolute, but is soft, squishy and negotiable."[1] —PETER KREEFT

One generation ago (1973), a few men in black robes decided that some persons, no matter how small, aren't persons. Since then, the progressive slide into the pit of moral relativism, confusion, inconsistency, hypocrisy, and evil has been ominously precipitous to the point today that legalizing ex-utero . . . *ahem* . . . abortion (i.e., infanticide) is being seriously discussed. The spirit of relativism and obfuscation lies heavy in the air . . . like a very toxic swamp gas.

Welcome to the Brave New World Disorder.

———

Roe with us into the quagmire,
Wade in this Immoral Pit.
Welcome to the Po-Mo Swampland,
Where confusion never quits.

Virtue's now been deconstructed.
Good means only what you "feel" . . .
When you say that you're "expecting,"
Friend, today that's no big deal!

You can always get around it . . .
It's a Brave New World, you see!
You can always take or leave it . . .
Po-Mo Ambiguity.

It's a fetus . . . No! A person!
Hold yer horses! Take that back!
That's no baby . . . But it's murder!
(I'm confused and can't keep track!)

OK, friend, let's keep our heads here . . .
Let's let Reason rule at last:
Weekends we will call it "Baby"
And on weekdays 'Tissue Mass."

Yep, on Monday name it "Cell-Growth,"
But on Sunday it's a Boy!
Tuesday/Wednesday it's "the Problem,"
But on Saturday a "Joy"!

Whoops! An "Accident" on Thursday,
And on Friday "Precious Child" . . .
Yes, I know, it's so confusing,
But, at last, it's reconciled!

Yes, my friend . . . I think we've got it!
That's the perfect compromise!
This way everybody's happy!
(More than that, extremely wise!)

This is great! We've solved "the Problem" . . .
Some days "what's" and some days "who's"!
Meet the New Age Bio-Ethics . . .
We believe! What's there to lose!?

Now *"Whatever!"* is our mantra—
Yep, it solves most everything!
It makes Truth obscure and fuzzy . . .
BUT it's got a pleasant ring!

———————

Vulgar relativism is an invisible gas, odorless, deadly, that is now polluting every free society on earth. It is a gas that attacks the central nervous system of moral striving. The most perilous threat to the free society today is, therefore, neither political nor economic. It is the poisonous, corrupting culture of relativism.[2]
—MICHAEL NOVAK

IT'S AN IVORY-TOWERED COUP

> We are all capable of believing things which we *know* to be untrue, and then, when we are finally proved wrong, impudently twisting the facts so as to show that we were right. Intellectually, it is possible to carry on this process for an indefinite time: the only check on it is that sooner or later a false belief bumps up against solid reality, usually on a battlefield.[1] —GEORGE ORWELL

———

Perfect trickle-down disaster . . .
Nihilism on display.
Is there really any wonder
We've completely lost our way?

It's a top-down form of cancer,
It's an iv'ry-towered coup.
It's a Golden Calf revival
Closing in on me and you.

It's the Plague of higher critics,
From the scoffers of the Word . . .
We were warned, but no one listened,
Now we're stuck with the absurd.

Poison gas of Humanism,
True light abolitionists.
Proudly roaring down the broad way
Toward the brink of this Abyss.

BREATHING IN THOSE NOXIOUS FUMES

"The human race is just a chemical scum on a moderate-sized planet,"[1] —STEPHEN HAWKING

"There is darkness without and when I die there will be darkness within. There is no splendor, nor vastness anywhere; only triviality for a moment and then nothing."[2] —BERTRAND RUSSELL

Peter Singer, Ethics Department Chair at Princeton University, predicts that "by 2040 . . . only a rump of hard-core, know-nothing religious fundamentalists will defend the view that every human life, from conception to death, is sacrosanct."[3]

The cult of metaphysical naturalism has become today's mandated cultural ideology. It's the golden calf around which lofty academics and their institutions must dance. Its drumbeat is required. It is a nihilistic gas. Several generations now have been breathing in its noxious fumes. This conceptual black hole of godless reason, proudly bred and nurtured in the highest echelons of academia, now permeates every aspect of Western culture, and today we are paying the murderously suicidal consequences.

Pastor and author Douglas Wilson notes that

> if there is no God, then all abstractions are chemical epiphenomena, like swamp gas over fetid water. This means that we have no reason for assigning truth and falsity to the chemical fizz we call reasoning or right and wrong to the irrational reaction we call morality. If no God, mankind is a set of bi-pedal carbon units of mostly water. And nothing else.[4]

Mass delusion breeds mass murder.
Nihilism, death, and pain.
When those dots go unconnected,
Watch the senseless terror reign.

Mindless mayhem making headway.
Bloody bedlam? . . . Glorified.
Firm foundations turned to rubble.
Self, our Sovereign, deified.

We've been singing Singer's swan song—
Seems to me we're almost done.
Now we're viewing human nature
Down the barrel of a gun.

It's all very "scientific."
Every PhD agrees!
Be a Nietzschean Avenger . . .
Suit Thy Self. . . . Do as you please!

If there really is no Purpose,
(As we must be taught in school)
If we're really only pond scum,
Mass bloodletting makes the rules.

If the bottom line is Nothing,
There's no Virtue to defend.
You can be the "god" that isn't!
The Beginning and the End.

I mean, really, what's the difference?
Who's to say what's "right" or "wrong"?
Kid, from one scum to another,
Nietzsche knew it all along.

Be the Hero of Indifference,
Show the world how much you care!
Free 'n' Famous on the dark web
While we glorify despair.

————

" . . . feels good to be free. I just love Hobbs [*sic*] and Nietzsche. Well tomorrow I'll buy 10 more round clips for my carbine . . ." —ERIC HARRIS (COLUMBINE SHOOTER'S DIARY)

IT'S WHY KLEBOLD PULLED THE TRIGGER

The Florida State University professor, influential evolutionary naturalist, and philosopher Michael Ruse has stated boldly that

> morality is a biological adaptation no less than hand and feet and teeth. Considered as a rationally justifiable set of claims about an objective something, ethics is illusory. . . . Morality is just an aid to survival and reproduction . . . and any deeper meaning is illusory.[1]

The young Columbine shooters Eric Harris and Dylan Klebold were in agreement: "Just because your mommy and daddy tell you blood and violence is bad, you think it's a [expletive] . . . ing law of nature? wrong only science and math are true, and I mean every [expletive] . . . ing else is manmade." (Eric Harris, diary)

Ideas have consequences.

———

Good's a simple "adaptation,"
Just a biologic fact.
Good's a thing that keeps evolving.
Too bad! . . . There's no looking back!

Good's progressing rather nicely . . .
Good's just chemistry, my friend.
Evil, too, is an illusion.
These are good points to defend!

It's why "ought" should be abolished . . .
Why "should" ought to be as well.
On that broad way to Whatever
Where true Virtue's been expelled.

It's why Klebold pulled the trigger,
And why Harris did the same.
It's why good bleeds into evil
And why no one is to blame.

It's the way of least resistance.
It's the ruse that feels just fine.
It's the path we took from Eden
On our way to Columbine.

WE WERE THERE TO RECLAIM EDEN

Twenty-five years after Woodstock, in August 1994, David Gates made the following comments in *Newsweek* magazine:

> The Dionysiac triad of sex, drugs and rock and roll now dominates private life and popular culture. The Aquarian tenet of radical egalitarianism informs much of our public and private discourse. Although few people outside the AMA actually talk like government-off-our-backs hippie anarchists anymore, the principle that laws are for killjoys has been put into practice everywhere from the inner city to Wall Street.... To a degree that would astonish a time traveler from 1969, we now live in Woodstock Nation. And ain't we got fun.[1]

In the summer of 1969, the Woodstock music festival in upstate New York unfolded before the eyes of the nation and the world.

The youthful "revolution" was officially on . . .

It started out, of course, all sunshine, flowers, and high "We-can-save-the-world!" utopian expectations.

It ended up somewhat differently, however.

Today, the 1960s Woodstock "All-you-need-is-love," Wavy-Gravy visionaries have been governing, teaching, and preaching (via Hollywood and the arts and higher education and from the more "progressive" pulpits) with unbridled passion and commitment, . . . and they have been doing deep.

These "visionaries" have become "The Establishment." They are the cultural elite, the worldly-wise, and the fashionably enlightened trendsetters of the day. Their influence has for more than a generation spread, high and low, like an invisible, odorless, and conscience-searing[2] toxic gas throughout the now highly evolved postmodernist realm.

The "Do-your-own-thing!" thing has been dutifully chiseled, commandment-like, in stone, passed down and passed around like an idol rite of pagan passage, or a doobie that we've all inhaled.

The narcissistic Mantra of Self has become THE cultural paradigm . . . NOT TO BE TAMPERED WITH(!).

The incongruous notion of pop lawless legalism and boundary-less, individual subjectivism has been codified and ingrained. The subsequent moral confusion has been culturally catastrophic.

Yet, still . . . the roots grow deeper and the beat goes on . . .

———————

Woodstock, man, held all answers,
We arrived to save the day . . .
We were high on Self (awareness?),
And, like, Wow! . . .We'd have our way!

"Progress" via pure emotion,
Feeling fine, the children reigned . . .
We were there to reclaim Eden,
Cosmic Campers quite unchained.

Down the tracks the Peace Train Cometh . . .
My, oh my! . . . We did our thing!
Peace 'n' Love our Declaration . . .
Fun 'n Games! . . . An endless fling!

We knew "All you need is Luv, man!"
We knew "free stuff" grew on trees!
We knew human hearts were lovely . . .
We would change Reality.

Woodstock Nation! . . .Yes! We made it! . . .
Mother Earth, at last be blessed!
When we looked back at the end, though . . .
All we made was just a mess.

We were blinded by emotion,
Feelings, too . . . and youthful Pride . . .
Foolish rebels from our fathers,
Lemmings with no place to hide.

Yasgur's field of green was ruined . . .
And his farm a sea of mud,
Yes, we left the place a trash heap . . .
Our Utopia? . . . A dud.

———————

Father, please have mercy on us!
Give us eyes again to see!
Show us Jesus, . . . Why He came here.[3]
Show us Grace at Calvary.

———————

"Then he spit on the ground, made mud with the saliva, and spread the mud over the blind man's eyes. He told him, 'Go wash yourself in the pool of Siloam' (Siloam means 'sent'). So the man went and washed and came back seeing!" (JOHN 9:6–7 NLT)

As Jesus approached Jericho, a blind beggar was sitting beside the road. When he heard the noise of a crowd going past, he asked what was happening. They told him that Jesus the Nazarene was going by. So he began shouting, "Jesus, Son of David, have mercy on me!"

"Be quiet!" the people in front yelled at him.

But he only shouted louder, "Son of David, have mercy on me!"

When Jesus heard him, he stopped and ordered that the man be brought to him. As the man came near, Jesus asked him, "What do you want me to do for you?"

"Lord," he said, "I want to see!"

And Jesus said, "All right, receive your sight! Your faith has healed you." Instantly the man could see, and he followed Jesus, praising God. And all who saw it praised God, too. (LUKE 18:35–43 NLT)

BOWING LOW TO OUR LIBIDO

"In those days there was no king in Israel; everyone did what was right in his own eyes." (JUDGES 21:25 NASB)

"It is a poverty to decide that a child must die so that you may live as you wish."[1] —MOTHER TERESA

———

On January 22, 2020, the nation "celebrated" the 47th anniversary of the Supreme Court's "Roe v. Wade" decision. Since that fateful day in 1973, an estimated sixty-two million souls in the United States have been denied the choice to live. Sixty-two million tiny bearers of God's image have been eradicated. All of the deaths were sanctioned and approved by Big Brother. Since that time in 1973, abortion "rights" have progressively expanded. What was advertised and sold to be "rare, safe, and legal," has today become an anytime, anyplace, and for any reason sacred rite.

The worldview and wisdom of radical secularism, the "acid reign" of humanism, has eaten away the moral foundation of Western civilized society. Today our culture receives its moral instruction not from Holy Scripture and three thousand years of Judeo-Christian tradition but instead from revived pagan high places: mainstream media, liberal scholars of higher learning, pop culture entertainment, social media, and various other hedonistic haunts.

The nation's conscience has been effectively seared. The borders of true morality have been breached. The fences are down and the floodgates are open. Any mention of traditional and objective morality is routinely shouted down by impassioned zealots of nihilism and various other strains of postmodernism's intelligentsia caste.

The apostle Paul foresaw this travesty nearly two millennia ago:

"The Spirit clearly says that in later times some will abandon the faith and follow deceiving spirits and things taught by demons. Such teachings come through hypocritical liars, whose consciences have been seared as with a hot iron." (1 TIMOTHY 4:1–2)

If it feels good, we say "Do it!"
It's the Woodstock Way, my friend.
Hedonism has its merits;
We're progressive to the End.

We embrace the sensate culture.
We fought hard for these delights!
To the barricades we're marching!
To abort's a human right!

Just ignore that ancient teaching,
Sacred Law? . . . Set that aside.
Bowing low to our Libido,
In the flesh we now abide.

Life's too precious to be squandered.
We believe in feeling good!
What else is there? . . . (I mean *really!?*)
What we want replaces *should.*

Now the fires of lust are kindled,
Sons and daughters sacrificed.
Right and wrong? . . . If that's an issue,
Tiny ones must pay the price.

We're the seared and liberated,
We've removed the bound'ry stones.
In No Border Land we're living;
There's not much we don't condone.

Roe v. Wade has now released us
From three thousand years of chains!
We're quite done with feeling "guilty". . .
New Age Humanism reigns!

———————

Father, how can You forgive us?
Sin has left our conscience numb . . .
May those tiny sacrifices
Make us bow before Your Son.

———————

To silence the voice that reminds us of our guilt is always the 'final solution' . . . self-exoneration is the genius of reason in its bent toward irrationality. There is no limit to which the mind will not stoop for cover when wanting to appear justified.[2] —RAVI ZACHARIAS

ARE THE CONSEQUENCES CLEAR YET?

"Where a society mistakes license for liberty, and establishes the Cult of the Imperial Self as its religion, the poor and vulnerable suffer."[1] —ROBERT P. GEORGE

Ideas have consequences.

When the heralded writings of Alfred Kinsey intruded into the consciousness of the Western world, the fuse was officially lit. The subsequent destructive "Big Bang" bombshell exploded dramatically in the 1960s, and the aftershocks are still expanding rapidly today . . . unabated.

The resulting spiritual debris of Self-indulgent hedonism is widespread and painfully obvious. And the toxic cup of iniquity is growing fuller by the day[2] . . .

Time to buckle up.

———————

When we "hooked-up," who-duh-thunk-it,
When we "liberated" sex,
That we'd still be making "progress"
With each pornographic text?

When the "All You Need Is Love" crowd
Was ecstatic with delight,
Did we see the train wreck coming
Through the dark, encroaching night?

When Pandora's box was opened
To the tune of "Let It Be,"
Did Utopiates among us
See the coming tragedy?

Did we see the evolution?
Did we note the slipp'ry slope?
Did we opt for "Well, whatever . . ."
And abandon future Hope?

Did we recognize the danger?
Or the Madness up ahead?
The delusion? . . . The confusion?
Western culture left for dead?

With Abortion Rites now sacred,
Pink Hat Habits now abound.
Friend, watch closely . . . Holy Scripture
Being driven underground.

Are the consequences clear yet
In the night clubs and the pews?
Are we searching for the Truth yet?[3]
For Eternity's Good News?

MAJORING IN FANCY FREE

Mottoes of America's first universities:

Harvard: "Veritas" ("Truth")

Dartmouth: "Vox clamantis in deserto" ("The voice of one crying in the wilderness")

Columbia: "In lumine tuo videbemus lumen" ("By the light, we see light")

Princeton: "Dei sub numine viget" ("Under the power of God she thrives")

Yale: "Lux et Veritas" ("Light and Truth")

———

Disregard old timey mottoes
That no longer mean much now.
Just matriculate with Gaia . . .
Come on in . . . we'll show you how.

Watch the a-theistic flourish
And the nonsense proudly sown.
Welcome to the New Age campus . . .
Self-ish Egos overgrown.

Just ignore time-tested classics,
Give veracity the boot.
Major in postmodern studies
So the past you may refute.

Undermine the Western Culture
You despise so thoroughly.
Cultivate deep-seeded anger.
Leave behind your sanity.

Proudly mock the Holy Scriptures . . .
Dig into the Dark Domain.
Make believe Truth's "unenlightened,"
Then complain, complain, complain.

Save yourself through good intentions,
Proudly disregard the past.
Keep demanding more attention . . .
Save the world . . . And do it fast!

FOLLOWERS OF FASHION

The Spirit of the Age . . . is always changing. It is subject to time and is changed by it. The literal meaning of *zeitgeist* is Time-Spirit. One who serves the Time-Spirit is one who wants to seem relevant to the fads and fashions of his own day. He is primarily concerned with being up-to-date. The problem is that those who are up-to-date are very soon out of date because, as C.S. Lewis quipped, fashions are always coming and going, but mostly going. One who is relevant to the fashions of today will be irrelevant to the fashions of tomorrow.[1] —JOSEPH PEARCE

We're the Followers of Fashion,
Up-to-Daters just in Time.
We're addicted now to "progress". . .
Progress is our Bottom Line.

If it changes, we're on board, sir.
We're just goin' with the flow . . .
We're not so much into anchors,
And our motto's "Like, ya know . . . ?"

We think wind was made for chasing.
We're the Zeitgeist Gals 'n' Guys.
We've got faith that Change will save us,
And that Truth should be "Revised."

THERE'S A GOULD-ISH NIGHTMARE BREWING

As paleontologist Dr. Mark McMenamin of Mt. Holyoke College admits,

> It's hard for us paleontologists, steeped as we are in a tradition of Darwinian analysis, to admit that neo-Darwinian explanations for the Cambrian explosion have failed miserably. New data acquired in recent years, instead of solving Darwin's dilemma, have rather made it worse.[1]

Charles Darwin knew from the outset that his theory of gradual evolutionary change could and would be challenged by the inconvenient truth presented by the Cambrian explosion of animal life. In fact, he was uncertain his theory would be able to stand in its light.

When in the early 1970s Stephen Jay Gould realized that the mechanism of incremental, gradual change proposed by the long-accepted paradigm of neo-Darwinian macro-evolutionism was inadequate to account for the Cambrian explosion of life forms, he posited his alternative scenario of rapid-fire (i.e., "punctuated") change. He called his theory "punctuated equilibrium" (or "Punk Eek"). He knew the Punk Eek scenario *must* have happened because the existing fossil record and the relatively short time span involved simply demanded it. The gradualism of undirected micro-change and adaptation was inadequate and untenable and could not explain the explosive diversity evident in the Cambrian fossil record. In effect, Gould's theory confirmed the validity of Darwin's doubt.

When Gould's Punk-Eek scenario was placed on the table for scrutiny and consideration in the early 1970s, the standardized mechanism of gradual macro-evolutionary change was called into question, and the distress flag began rising up the credibility flagpole of traditional neo-Darwinian thinking.

Then later, when it was discovered and confirmed that mountains of complex, specified information had to be encoded into the molecular/genetic makeup of living animals in order for such morphological diversity to occur during the Cambrian era, the distress flag was raised higher still. After all, common sense and daily observation testify that specified information always originates from an *intelligent* source. But, alas, the possibility of an intelligent, designing agent had to be ruled out because intelligent agents in contemporary Macro-Evolutionville are not allowed to exist.

Unbiased science simply demands to have the final word. And whatever unbiased Science says is always so.

So, where did all that specified information encoded into our genes come from? How was it installed, implanted, and/or programmed? In response to the obvious questions, we are told emphatically: "Don't ask."(Ask us no questions, we'll tell you no lies.)

Yet despite this hard-boiled, unscientific attitude, mindless methodological naturalism, the long-accepted, undirected *modus operandi* of materialist presupposition, *is* now being called into question by more and more honest, truth-seeking scientists. Predictably, Darwinian high priests of philosophical scientism are frightened by this new scientific honesty and inquisitiveness . . . just as they are spooked by the possibility of having to accept the reality of Intelligent Design as a scientifically viable consideration and theory.

And the Pharisees of scientism are howling.

According to Dr. Russell Carlson, professor of biochemistry and molecular biology at the University of Georgia,

[B]ased on cutting-edge molecular biology . . . explaining the origin of animals is now not just a problem of missing fossils, but an even greater engineering problem at the molecular level . . . the neo-Darwinian mechanism cannot produce the genetic information needed to build new animals.[2]

———————

Darwin's doubt is back to haunt 'em,
Like a phantom shadow cast.
Macro-evolution's story . . .
Like a specter fading fast.

Yes, the witch's brew is cooling . . .
It's diluting, getting weak . . .
Some can sense the spell is broken,
Darwin's Cauldron's sprung a leak.

There's a casket in the corner . . .
And a stake right through the heart.
If you listen very closely,
You might hear the rasping start.

There's a scuff'ling on the front porch,
There's a bumping in the night,
Chains are rattl'ing in the attic . . .
In the cellar there's a fright.

It's a Gould-ish nightmare brewing,
Quite a horror to behold!
You can hear punks out there "Eeeek-ing!"
As the Awe-ful Truth unfolds.

Yes, the Cambrian Explosion
Has been proved a ghastly tale.
They're still falling over fossils
Never found in Burgess Shale.

Seems that Darwin's explanation,
Has some holes too big to fill,
It's quite grave and getting deeper.
For some, *that's* a bitter pill!

Now the Trick or Treat conundrum
Is a terror for them all.
Truth is always hard to swallow
When you're up against a wall.

You can sense increasing panic:
"No I.D.! . . . You must desist!"
In their Boo-Who paranoia . . .
You can see 'em writhe 'n' twist.

You can see 'em start to quiver,
Watch 'em glare then watch 'em shake!
Darwin's doubt is out there stalking,
And it's keeping them awake.

———————

... [T]his Darwinian claim to explain all of evolution is a popular half-truth whose lack of explicative power is compensated for only by the religious ferocity of its rhetoric . . . No evidence in the vast literature of heredity changes shows unambiguous evidence that random mutation itself, even with geographical isolation of populations, leads to speciation.[3] —LYNN MARGULIS, BIOLOGIST AND PRESIDENTIAL MEDAL OF SCIENCE WINNER

WHERE THE HATTER JUST GETS MADDER

nihilism: n.

> 1 a. the denial of the existence of any basis for
>   knowledge or truth
>   b. the general rejection of customary beliefs in morality,
>   religion, etc.
> 2. the belief that there is no meaning or purpose
>   in existence

(WEBSTER'S NEW WORLD DICTIONARY)

———

"Who gave us the sponge to wipe away the entire horizon? What did we do when we unchained the earth from
its sun?"[1] —FRIEDRICH NIETZSCHE ("THUS SPAKE ZARATHUSTRA")

———

> Take the Sponge of Deconstruction,
> Son, just wipe away the sky!
> Never mind the consequences . . .
> Never bother asking "Why?"

———

Well over a century ago, Friedrich Nietzsche recognized the metaphysical writing on the wall. He was ahead of his time. Today his
dark, prophetic vision is rapidly unfolding before us.

His vision has a name today: postmodern deconstructionism. *It is a rootless, truthless, and ruthless philosophical paradigm.* Its "bottom line" declares proudly that there is no Bottom Line at all. All traditional, unifying categories of reality, order, virtue, right, and reason are being shattered into meaningless, psychological smithereens in its despairing and disparaging wake.

Nietzsche's nihilism is in full, self-destructive, chaotic "bloom." His Zarathustra saw it coming . . .

Carl Trueman, a contemporary theologian, has observed that once the "categories of identity are [declared] merely psychological and that reality is constituted by language"[2] (i.e., the deconstructionist's main meme), we have, indeed, become "unchained." Trueman goes on to say,

> Those who accept its premises and yet seek to curb its power according to their own tastes are merely so many desperate postmodern[s] . . . shouting impotently at the relentless waves of ecstatic nihilism that are even now crashing against the shore.[3]

This is where grim Fairy Tale and Wonderland intersect with and then are swallowed up by hopeless nightmare.

Watch the Real and True receding,
In the dark Postmodern mist . . .
Where the Tribe of Dissolution's
Ruled by dim immoralists.

Here's where Mr. Dumpty's reigning,
Here the floodgates open wide . . .
Here the Hatter just gets Madder,
And there's no "Safe Place" to hide.

It's the fruit of Nietzsche's Notion,
In the world of "Let's Pretend!"
It's delusion at its darkest,
Where the Light of Truth offends.

Yes, it's Zarathustra's Tarpit
In the NeverLand of Pan.
It's where Lost Boys are exalted,
And the devil's in command.

———————

Lord, You've given us the Promise.
Yes, despite our broken loss . . .
Give us Light to know the Way now
To the Anchor of the Cross.[4]

———————

Now when he heard that John had been arrested, [Jesus] withdrew into Galilee. And leaving Nazareth he went and lived in Capernaum by the sea, in the territory of Zebulun and Naphtali, so that what was spoken by the prophet Isaiah might be fulfilled:

"The land of Zebulun and the land of Naphtali,
　　the way of the sea, beyond the Jordan,
　　　　Galilee of the Gentiles—
the people dwelling in darkness
　　have seen a great light,
and for those dwelling in the region and shadow
　　　　of death,
　　on them a light has dawned."

(MATTHEW 4:12–16 ESV)

TEACHING KIDS TO PICK THEIR GNOSIS

"Some ideas are so stupid only intellectuals believe them."[1] —GEORGE ORWELL

"I have sometimes fancied that, as chilly people like a warm room, silly people sometimes like a diffused atmosphere of intellectualism and long words."[2] —G. K. CHESTERTON

Unchained idol humanism has its roots sunk deep into the upper-crusted, rarified air of Western academia, so much so that it has left an entire generation breathless in its wake.

Recently, we have learned that (once again) the high priests of postmodern logic and deconstructed reason have proven that their highly touted agenda has been exposed as something . . . (shall we say?) . . . "less than honest."

No joke.

It was recently reported that a trio of academics submitted an array of purposely meaningless papers to various professional journals for consideration. Apparently, many of the submitted papers met the high standards of the peer-reviewers and were published.[3] (Another Sokal Hoax?[4])

Nonsensical linguistic drivel in, nonsensical linguistic drivel out . . .

Just when you think the ivy-covered ivory tower of Babble could not possibly rise any higher, someone adds another course of bogus postmodern bricks.

One might hope, as the academic nonsense reaches new stratospheric heights, that Big Brother, the Emperor of Higher Ed, would recognize that this naked philosophical sham ought to be rolled back in the name of common decency. Tragically, however, the proud pied pipers of New Age progressivism keep parading on, and the culture follows blindly—and eagerly—into the slough of toxic, graceless grievance.

Lord, have mercy.

———————

We've got extra special Gnosis,
Gnosis that you need to know.
Pseudo-scientific Gnosis—
Nonsense Gnosis grow and grow.

We're Most High-ly educated,
Here to tell you what to do.
We've got secret highbrow Gnosis
That we're looking down on you.

Majoring in "Outer Darkness,"
Dream the dream you feel is best.
Find the Hoax you can be proud of,
Minor in thy "Gnostic Quest."

Teaching kids to pick their Gnosis,
Find your truth, and Let It Be!
Digging deeper mass, hip Gnosis . . .
Earn your Grievance PhD.

Get in line . . . Get educated!
Put that "Doctor" by your name!
Get yourself Utopiated!
College of No Blame or Shame.

———

"Whoever walks with the wise becomes wise, but the companion of fools will suffer harm." (PROVERBS 13:20 ESV)

THE HEMINGWAY IS HERE TO STAY

Ernest Hemingway, swaggering hero of the mid-twentieth century literary avant-garde, had everything the world had to offer: talent, pleasure, fame, fortune, and high adventure.

All that was missing, apparently, was purpose, . . . a moral Anchor for the Self-centered soul.

In 1961, the ribald, macho, swashbuckling, no-holds-barred "man's man" took his own life. Alcohol, frustration, pent-up unresolved anger, despair, and depression eventually took their toll.

A life lived without the true knowledge of God will eventually be proved empty . . . a meaningless vapor on the wind.

Imagine a number of men in chains, all under penalty of death, some of whom are each day butchered in the sight of others. Those remaining see their own condition in that of their fellows, and looking at each other with grief and despair await their turn. This is an image of the human condition.[1] —BLAISE PASCAL

"Another form of despair [is] running from the truth of death. It does not succeed in avoiding death, only in avoiding truth."[2] —PETER KREEFT

"There's no one thing that is true. They're all true."[3] —ERNEST HEMINGWAY

"What is moral is what you feel good after. What is immoral is what you feel bad after."[4] —ERNEST HEMINGWAY

———

The Hemingway's
Still on display . . .
Sophisticates of doom.
His lemming way
Is here to stay.
It's where the darkness looms.

He understood
That "feeling good"
Defines for us what's right . . .
That lech'rous stand
And leprous hand
Have ushered in this blight.

The body? . . . Cold.
The bell has tolled . . .
His sun did also set.
The Lie he brayed,
Big Game he played . . .
Then finally lost his bet.

We've joined the crowd . . .
The loud and proud,
So Sin we all can hide.
A dark mistake,
A nightmare wake,
A culture's suicide.

So "Cheers!" to you!
Let's down a few
Straight existential shots.
It's understood,
Right's feelin' good!
And hopelessness our plot.

El Toro, man!
In Nietszche-Land,
Drinks deep from glasses full!
He staggered there
In his despair . . .
Was gored by his own bull.

The Nihilist still shakes his fist,
And trusts grim fairy tales . . .
But soon he sees
The soul's disease:
Death's whiter shade of pale.

———————

Lord, we re-hearse
This Fallen Curse,
That drives us to the grave.
But now by Grace
Through Faith we taste
The Truth that Jesus saves!

We've heard You say,
We've lost our way . . .
And that You hold the Key.
Yet we still scoff,
And put You off . . .
And say, "I'm trusting Me!"

The Hemingway
Is here to stay.
The Fall's what Adam chose.
But now we see,
Bright Calvary . . .
The Son Who Also Rose.

The Grace He brings
To mankind sings
Of Glory, Hope, and Love.
The story told
Grows never old . . .
This Plot is from Above.

———————

"We who have fled to take hold of the hope set before us may be greatly encouraged. We have this hope as an anchor for the soul, firm and secure. It enters the inner sanctuary . . . , where our forerunner, Jesus, has entered on our behalf." (HEBREWS 6:18B–20A)

CLOSE YOUR EYES AND MAKE IT HAPPEN

"At the heart of liberty is the right to define one's own concept of existence, of meaning, of the universe, and of the mystery of human life."[1] —ANTHONY KENNEDY

When in 1992 Chief Justice Anthony Kennedy penned those fateful words in a Supreme Court decision that confirmed and expanded abortion "rights," the dictatorship of relativism and the sacred reign of the Autonomous Self were confirmed. The first commandment of the religion of fundamentalist secular humanism was finally and authoritatively etched in stone.

And, today, the beat goes on . . .

It's the essence of rebellion.[2]
It's the Devil's Paradigm . . .
We're in charge of Truth and Meaning,
Law and Justice . . . even Crime.

We decide what's true for us now.
We dream up what's really Real!
Close your eyes and make it happen.
Keep the Faith in what you feel.

Welcome to the Roe we're sowing,
And the tarpit where we Wade.
Welcome to this present darkness
And the True Light we evade.

Welcome to Mass Deconstruction,
Welcome to the New Age Game.
Welcome to the Swamp of Nonsense
Where we all outsmarted shame.

Welcome to the Void we fell for . . .
Humanism now enthroned.
Where what's "moral" is subjective,
There's not much we won't condone.

Welcome to the "Well . . . , Whatever!"
Welcome to the grave we've dug.
Welcome to the strong delusion
Where the Truth's swept under rugs.

THE GALAPAGOS STING

"The ship [evolutionary materialism] has sprung a metaphysical leak, and the leak widens as more and more people understand it and draw attention to the conflict between empirical science and materialist philosophy."[1] —PHILLIP JOHNSON

Just a little fun with the cultural hearse drivers of Western civilization, the dogmatic fundamentalists in the materialist-naturalism camp of religious scientism, who—without excuse—continue to bark up St. Darwin's Idola-Tree.

———————

The Galapagos Sting
Where Lord Darwin is King
And his Word is the Law of the land.
Evolution's defenders,
The Inherit the Wind-ers
Have drawn their hard line in the sand.

Though the theory's quite hollow,
Still the children must swallow
Their soup cooked up pre-biotic.
Yes, the game to defame
God's Word is a shame,
"Good intentions" uniquely Quixotic.

Now the gospel's demoted,

Evo-Priests have all noted

That those miracles simply can't be!

Eyes and minds tightly closed

Revelation's opposed . . .

Dogmatists barking up a dead tree.

This is Science . . . and Reason!

Faulty logic's in season,

Lucky mud over time . . . *Man alive!*

A Designer? . . . Oh, please!

Sir, get up from your knees!

In this land only top dogs survive.

While the culture's kow-towing,

All the children are bowing

At Darwin's gold Altar of Chance.

It's the Faith with no head,

Evolution's the Bread . . .

And the wine that we sip?

Happenstance.

Their Cosmology's queer,

But their Creed's crystal clear . . .

To this Faith they're uniquely devoted.

They're High Priests on the go

Who just want you to know

That we're here because Nothing exploded.

Yes, their Origin Tale
Has been growing more stale.
It's a Dogma that some know is doomed.
It's the Great Contradiction,
A Unique Science Fiction . . .
The Religion of *Nothing went BOOM!*

Since that Bang, which was BIG,
They continue to dig
To find missing links that aren't there.
Priests of Darwin quite sure
That their Faith is secure
With their feet planted (Proud) in thin air.

————

"In the beginning God . . . ." (GENESIS 1:1)

"In the beginning was the Word, and the Word was
with God, and the Word was God. He was in the beginning with God. All things were made through him, and
without him was not any thing made that was made.
In him was life, and the life was the light of men. The
light shines in the darkness, and the darkness has not
overcome it." (JOHN 1:1–5 ESV)

HAWKING OUR ESCAPE PLAN

> Today, faith is more often channeled through science. Not only the pseudo-science of crop circle enthusiasts and UFO cultists, but genuine advances in science and technology are being used to promote hopes and dreams that are quintessentially religious.[1] —JOHN GRAY

Shortly before his death in 2018, Stephen Hawking proclaimed in true Malthusian panic-driven hysteria mode that humanity had only one hundred years to plan and execute our escape from planet Earth in order to avoid future impending destruction, extinction, and existential doom.

Apparently, the religion of metaphysical scientism has its own enlightened version of the rapture.

————

One more time: "The sky is falling!"
Scientism has her say.
Screwtape's hawking our escape route
Retro-fitted for today.

Chicken Little makes a comeback.
Tell us we won't surely die![2]
Teach us to avoid destruction.
What's this new plan we should try?

Our religion? . . . "Settled Science"
Re-imagined as we please.
Only we can really save us
From those "Good Book" heresies.

————

Humanism's Plan of Action . . .
Man's salvation on our own.
"Naturalism" is the Word now
From the Mind of Man alone.

Substitutionary rapture . . .
It's the new good news we've heard.
Man retreats into the darkness.[3]
Dodging judgment . . . truth deferred.

THERE'S A PILE-UP ON THE BROAD WAY

When emotion overrules the head, when sentiment charts the course, when feelings captivate the mind, trouble is on the way. When "fairness" replaces truth and justice, and good intentions rule the roost, mass dysfunction is sure to follow, and bedlam lies in wait.

As C. S. Lewis explains:

> No emotion is, in itself, a judgement; in that sense all emotions and sentiments are alogical. But they can be reasonable or unreasonable as they conform to Reason or fail to conform. The heart never takes the place of the head: but it can, and should, obey it.[1]

———

The Emotionals are winning,
The Subjectivists have gained,
The Utopiates are dreaming,
Mother Naturalists are pained.

Now the Touchies far outnumber
Those who stand with Ages Past.
And the Feelies are progressing
Straight downhill . . . and really fast!

There's a Sentimental Breakdown
In the Far Left lane, my friend,
There's a pile-up on the broad way
In this Realm of Just-Pretend.

Yes, The Tribalists are screaming,
And The Co-Existants chant.
Everybody's "extra-special."
(Common sense is extra-scant.)

Everybody's got their Group-on . . .
(It's a Selfie-thing, you see.)
After one more March of Madness . . .
Rest assured, we'll all agree.

Everybody gets a "safe place" . . .
(Except babies in the womb).
We feel blessed by contradictions
In the Land of Whitewashed Tombs.[2]

———

. . . [S]omewhere in the world of philosophy, we made a huge blunder across the centuries, when we lost contact with the reality of our emotions and made human beings purely cerebral. Then in the 1960's, the existentialist philosophers became so popular focusing on emotion, focusing on passion, focusing on experience, and swung the pendulum to the other side to where rationality was not as important as much as acting for the passion of the moment. Somewhere in the middle is the balance. . . . Emotions are supposed to be indicators of reality, not fabricators, or framers of reality.[3]
—RAVI ZACHARIAS

WE HAVE FAITH IN NOTHING REALLY!

Over the past few decades, there has been much excited chatter in certain inner circles and higher echelons of academia (mostly in university science and philosophy departments) about how the existence of "god" has been disproved, justifiably written off, and at last properly disposed of. With an air of omniscient finality, these academic experts have declared that belief in any type of divine creator, intelligent designer, and/or omnipotent being is no longer an acceptable intellectual position to hold, that God was never anything more than an outlandishly childish and primitive myth. "God," we are now authoritatively informed, is and always has been a fictitious intruder, a "crutch" foolishly imagined by the intellectually challenged. "God," they say, was simply an invented notion dreamed up so that the ignorant masses could cope sufficiently with the rigors of daily living. In full-fledged paternalistic mode, skeptics assert: God is no more real than Santa Claus, the Easter Bunny, the Tooth Fairy or . . . (and this is their favorite clever put-down du jour) . . . a flying spaghetti monster.[1]

The doubters have confirmed that science has at last proven God to be quite unnecessary, and that the universe (i.e., all space, time, light, matter, beauty, morality, creativity, love, and all the rest) in fact popped into existence from essentially nothing nowhere.

With a snap of their fingers, these high priests of philosophical scientism assigned "god" to the back of the bus, and then with a dismissive wave of the wand of metaphysical naturalism declared God to be *persona non grata* . . . POOF! God simply disappeared.

Shortly before his death, the theoretical physicist Stephen Hawking declared that it was, in fact, scientifically *inevitable* that the universe as we know it today would quite *naturally* pop up out of some sort of "gravitational fluctuation" of the empty void. Another top scholar, Lawrence Krauss, even wrote a book (*A Universe from* Nothing) about this mystical phenomenon. (And this author actually swears, even to this very day, that his book is not a work of fiction.)

These New Age, militant *neo-nihilistas* are the deep thinkers of contemporary materialism. They wield an extraordinary amount of power and influence in Western culture today. Despite the fact that their theories rest upon the absurd notion that everything came from nothing, they are feted and have become Western civilization's highly esteemed movers and shakers, blazing progressive trails deep into the sophisticated black holes of human reason.

These New Atheists (Albert Einstein once referred to this group as fanatical atheists) sincerely believe that everything just appeared out of nothing really, for really no reason at all!

In fact, the New Atheists' "god" seems to be, quite literally, "Nothing Really"—a void in a vacuum one rung lower on the scale of idol nonsense than the flying spaghetti monster herself.

They are committed to naturalism's pledge of allegiance: "Nobody times Nothing equals everything."

Nothing Really's Their Creator. (And to *Nothing* will they bow.)

––––––––––

We know "god's" not in the picture!
We know "god's" now been erased.
We know Nothing has created
Space and Time and *every* Place!

From a lotta *nada* nowhere,
Nothing's really truth, in fact!
We know Nothing's really something,
And we're all okay with that!

We swear Science really tells us
Nothing Really's really true!
We popped out of Nothing really . . .
We're convinced that you did, too!

Nothing really fluctuated . . .
Nothing really made it all . . .
Nothing really, *really* matters!
Not much, really, not at all.-

We have Faith in Nothing really.
We hold Nothing very dear.
Nothing Really has convinced us
Nothing's here between our ears!

Here's our own "Spaghetti Monster.". . .
Nothing Really! . . . Take a bow!
We invite you . . . Use your noodle!
Nothing answers why and how.

What? . . . You think we're onto something?
Oh, that's Nothing Really, friend!
Nothing Really gave us wisdom . . .
Nothing's what we comprehend.

———

That which does not exist only begins to exist through something already existing. Therefore, if at one time nothing was in existence, it would have been impossible for anything to have begun to exist, and thus even now nothing would be in existence which is absurd.[2]

—THOMAS AQUINAS

"Nothing comes from nothing. Nothing ever could."[3]

—RICHARD ROGERS

"'You, Lord, laid the foundation of the earth in the beginning, and the heavens are the work of your hands.'"

(HEBREWS 1:10 ESV)

PEER INTO THIS WELL, WHATEVER

When he whispered the infamous words to Eve: "Did God really say . . . ?" (Genesis 3:1), Satan became the first philosopher of deconstructionist logic, a system of thought that is enjoying a mass revival among the cultured intellectuals and ivory-towered philosophers of today. Of course, the spiritual juggernaut of relativism has been rolling through the ages here, East of Eden, for quite some time, but today's version is proving to be particularly virulent and potent.

The "philosophies of man" just keep on coming. Throughout recorded history, the variations on Satan's theme have been legion, but at its core the scheme has been consistently the same: appeal to pride and human autonomy via subtle deception.

In his epic poem *Paradise Lost,* John Milton puts the following words in the mouth of Satan: "The mind is its own place and in itself can make a heaven of hell, a hell of heaven."[1] When Milton penned this line in the seventeenth century, he penetrated to the heart of the matter. Long before the contemporary brand of the humanist project was spawned, Milton was in the know.

Come inside, friend, for a visit,
Please enjoy my point of view.
Look around, this is my heaven.
Though it may be hell to you.

That's OK . . . It's all subjective.
It's been proven . . . Rest assured!
We've progressed past "categories."
It's the new Postmodern Cure.

Here's the doorway to the Kingdom.
Feel the Truth . . . YOU are the Key!
Welcome to "It's Up-to-You-ville"!
Long live pure Autonomy!

You can trust us! . . .We've made *progress*!
We are all now Number One!
Free your Self! . . . Come on, just DO IT!
Grab the reins! . . . "Thy will be done!"

You might say it's just like magic!
Do your truth, and I'll do mine.
Peer into this "Well-Whatever"
Where we know no bottom line.

———————

"Don't let anyone capture you with empty philosophies
and high-sounding nonsense that come from human
thinking and from the spiritual powers of this world,
rather than from Christ." (COLOSSIANS 2:8 NLT)

ALL THOSE TINY LIVES IN NEWTOWN

The following words were spoken on December 16, 2012, by President Barack Obama in response to the tragic school shooting in Newtown, Connecticut:

> This is our first task—caring for our children. It's our first job. If we don't get that right, we don't get anything right. That's how, as a society, we will be judged. . . . And by that measure, can we truly say, as a nation, that we are meeting our obligations? Can we honestly say that we're doing enough to keep our children—all of them—safe from harm? Can we claim, as a nation, that we're all together there, letting them know that they are loved, and teaching them to love in return? Can we say that we're truly doing enough to give all the children of this country the chance they deserve to live out their lives in happiness and with purpose? . . . We can't accept events like this as routine. Are we really prepared to say that we're powerless in the face of such carnage, that the politics are too hard? Are we prepared to say that such violence visited on our children year after year after year is somehow the price of our freedom?[1]

All those tiny lives in Newtown,
Father God, how could this be . . . ?
Holy Spirit, help us fathom
This perverse atrocity!

Give us wisdom to discern, Lord . . .
Why this Evil? . . . Why this pain?
What's this war that we're detecting?
What's this battlefield campaign?

Is the issue really weapons?
Are the guns here, Lord, to blame?
Is it bullets? . . . Maybe triggers?
(Something tells me *that's* insane!)

Can Big Brother really fix us?
With another round of Law?
Or, perhaps, there's something deeper
In the soul . . . *A deadly flaw*?

Could it be we're missing something?
Have we fallen for the "spin"?
Tell the truth, Lord . . . We can take it!
Could the problem here be *Sin!?*

———————

Lord, have mercy! . . . What has happened!?
Haven't people realized?
O, Sweet Lord, *where is our conscience*?
Simply seared and cauterized.

All those little lives in Newtown!
God, they never had a prayer!
Only your Law now can help us,
This is more than we can bear!

All those little ones in Newtown
Multiplied now every day . . .
We don't see it . . . We don't feel it.
We've forgotten how to pray.

Father, give us Grace to hear You . . .
May we do so through your Son.
Take us to the Cross of Calv'ry . . .
Lord, we're blind to what we've done.

MR. NIETZSCHE SAW IT COMING

One hundred and fifty years ago, Friedrich Nietzsche, the god-father of "progressive" (and aggressive) postmodernism, proudly proclaimed that

> truths are illusions about which one has forgotten that this is what they are; metaphors which are worn out and without sensuous power; coins which have lost their pictures and now matter only as metal, no longer as coins.[1]

Today, the toxic effect of trickle-down nihilism has taken its toll. Nietzsche's philosophical poison gas has seeped into every corner of Western society.

Underlying acid rain.

Ideas have consequences.

Today, we are paying the piper.

———

> When the Truth's declared "illusion,"
> Watch emotion rule and reign.
> Disapproval turns to hatred,
> Watch the growing crimson stain.
>
> Mr. Nietzsche saw it coming
> Strapped in Bedlam long ago.
> Now his Nihilistic vision
> Is the liberal wind we sow.[2]

We're in finger-pointing free-fall,
There's no Rock, no solid ground.[3]
Humanism's own Creation . . .
Simply darkness all around.

That Progressive Pilate Program[4] . . .
Here it comes around again!
If you're able, hide the children
From the serpent's ancient spin.[5]

———————

If you've got a Bible handy,
Might be time to peek inside.
You may find the Living Word there[6]
Who exposes deadly pride.

You may find the Truth . . . Incarnate,
Yes, true Hope, and Joy . . . and more!
You may find Amazing Grace there . . .
And the Peace you're longing for.

DR. SINGER MAY BE SINGING

> Knowledge is a deadly friend
> If no one sets the rules.
> The fate of all mankind I see
> Is in the hands of fools.
> —KING CRIMSON[2]

Dr. Peter Singer, the Ira W. deCamp Chair of Bio-Ethics at Princeton University, has for years been preaching that human infants are in fact not really human persons at all and that choosing to "abort" members of this class of tiny sub-humans should not be considered immoral or unethical. Singer, a "speciesist" and former Green Party candidate who lost his grandparents in Nazi concentration camps, champions animal liberation but seems to have a problem with human babies. Whether they are *in utero* or *ex utero* seems not to matter much at all.

Singer suggests that perhaps it is time to shed three thousand years of Judeo-Christian moral teaching[3] (i.e., that human beings are created in the image of God) and to adopt the perspective that

> human babies are not born self-aware or capable of grasping their lives over time. They are not persons. Hence their lives would seem to be no more worthy of protection than the life of a fetus.[4]

He has made the case that human babies are no different, practically speaking, from farmyard animals. Whether Dr. Singer is suggesting that animals be officially elevated to human status (or "personhood") under law or that human beings be demoted to simple barnyard animal status is, I suppose, debatable. What is not debatable, however, is that Dr. Singer believes that infanticide may not be that bad . . . As he has so eloquently stated: "The position that allows abortion also allows infanticide under some circumstances. . . . If we accept abortion, we do need to rethink some of those more fundamental attitudes about human life."[5]

Singer has borrowed a page from Margaret Sanger's 1930s Darwinian Eugenics Songbook and has jazzed up the score for the more—(ahem)— "sophisticated" modern ear. Dr. Singer has been singing his radically discordant tune for some time, but recently his song has been getting more airtime. His views are now considered "respectable." They are today quite mainstream and are esteemed more and more by cloistered intelligentsia and liberal politicians. Just as one example, in a February 2012 article printed in the prestigious *Journal of Medical Ethics*, two scholars, Francesca Minerva and Alberto Giubilini, echoed Dr. Singer's thoughts. They made the case that both newborns and yet-to-be-born babies are not actual persons and are therefore morally irrelevant. In light of this "fact," they go on to make the case that post-birth abortion (i.e., infanticide) ought to be permissible. In the introduction of the article, they summarized their position this way:

> Abortion is largely accepted even for reasons that do not have anything to do with the fetus' health. By showing that (1) both fetuses and newborns do not have the same moral status as actual persons, (2) the fact that both are potential persons is morally irrelevant and (3) adoption is not always in the best interest

of actual people, the authors argue that what we call "after-birth abortion" (killing a newborn) should be permissible in all the cases where abortion is, including cases where the newborn is not disabled.[6]

And so, the Singer-Sanger roadshow is on. The New Age code of utilitarian ethics has evolved and now (predictably) has taken cultural center stage. The amps have been turned way, way up. The Singer-Sanger bandwagon has hit the slippery downslope of amorality. It has picked up speed and is now careening blindly toward moral chaos and mass delusion.

Apparently, the pagan beat of ancient Molech has made a comeback.

See that baby in the corner?
Her life won't be as it should!
I can tell she'll be a problem . . .
Yes, ma'am, it's just understood!

She's not really quite a "person";
And we're sure she's unaware.
Her life may not be worth living . . .
Let's abort and show we care.

She's just not what we'd call "human."
She's not really at that stage.
"Cute" enough, but just not woke yet . . .
Clueless and quite disengaged.

She has no real moral standing . . .
Not just yet, . . . and that's the glitch!
She's no diff'rent from a tomcat,
Or some little mongrel bitch.

We'll decide for you what's "human."
When a "what" becomes a "who"!
On these shifting sands of reason,
Moral Law we may undo.

"Higher Law" has been disproven . . .
Ma'am, we know about these things!
We've been schooled in Bio-Ethics,
Singing songs that Singer sings!

Listen to that song of Singer . . .
(Margaret Sanger sang it, too).
Jewish friends might recognize it;
That's because it's nothing new.

Prophet Orwell also heard it,
And at last now . . . here it comes!
Peter Singer may be singing,
But that's Molech on the drums.

Hear the downbeat? . . . That's Eugenics,
Euthanasia's Rhythm Band.
Heart of Mengele's still beating
On the stage of shifting sand.

Margaret Sanger's singing back-up
That's Kevorkian on bass . . .
Moral Chaos dancing proudly,
Mask of sneering grin in place.

———————

Lord, we know the score's demonic . . . ,
Plainly Molech's ancient song;
Conscience whispers, "This is Evil!"
Still, we all just hum along.

Lord, have mercy! Please forgive us!
By your Spirit, Heaven sent . . .
Help us see this darkness in us;
And our need, Lord, to repent.

Help us understand the message
Penned in Romans chapter three . . .
By your Word, Lord, there convict us!
Take us then to Calvary.

———————

"[Naturalism's] . . . attempted murder not of persons
but of personhood, not of humans but of humanness
itself. Naturalism will not succeed in its quest to kill.
That does not mean it is not trying."[7] —TOM GILSON

"Jesus said, 'Father, forgive them, for they do not know
what they are doing.'" (LUKE 23:34)

MULTIVERSES TO THE RESCUE!

When we analyzed the figures,
We thought Chance and Time would do . . .
But we couldn't fake the numbers, . . .
So we dreamed up something new!

Hmmm . . . , we pondered. Let's pretend here.
Make believe . . . That's better still!
Multiverses! . . . That's the answer!
Oh my, yes . . . That fits the bill!

We thought Chance 'n' Time could do it.
But the notion crashed and burned.
"Multiverses to the rescue!"
My-oh-my! So much to learn!

Though we've never really seen one . . .
And we don't know if they're there;
Still by Faith we just believe it . . .
Gospel Science fills the air.

Endless Mythic Multiverses . . .
Brooms 'n' Buckets . . . Come alive!
Hocus-pocus is our focus . . .
Fantasy in overdrive.

Yes, the Scientism Genie
Has at last moved in to stay!
Glory, glory . . . Hallelujah!
Science fiction saves the day!

Bowing to Almighty Matter . . .
Yes, our Hope's in Science now!
Naturalism is our Dogma,
Mind of Man our Sacred Cow.

———————

"Whoever has the authority to tell a culture's creation story functions as its de facto priesthood with the power to determine what the dominant worldview will be."[1]—NANCY PEARCEY

HERE IN BABEL WE HEAR PROFITS

Perhaps in some distant corner closet of the great towering monolith that is the abortion industry, there are people who genuinely are helping women. But the halls echo with silent screams. The walls are painted in antiseptic blood. If you look closely, the building is not made with stone or wood. The whole thing, including the modernized Planned Parenthood logo, is made of rotting bodies. It smells like death and it stinks like the valley where the worm does not die.[1] —OWEN STRACHAN

In 2015 Ms. Priscilla Smith, a lawyer (and a highly distinguished Yale graduate), testified before Congress on Capitol Hill on behalf of Planned Parenthood. She declared that dismembering babies during the abortion process was "very humane."[2]

To borrow from the liberated parlance of yesteryear, all I can say is, "We've come a long way, baby!" And not in a good way.

———

Here in Babel we hear Profits
Of a very different sort . . .
You can bet your bottom dollar,
We've got babies to abort.

Yes, Big Brother holds the purse strings,
There's less hope but lots of change!
Jeremiah may have warned us,
But God's Word's been re-arranged.

Just remember . . . we dismember
In the name of "Greater Good,"
We renamed it, sir, "compassion,"
In this dark Planned Parent hood.

There's tongue-wagging in the pulpits,
More hot air up on the Hill,
In the meantime, Molech snickers
While more tiny ones are killed.

Fed on fantasies, we wallow,
And with Asherah we dance.
We pay homage now to Darwin
And creation-happenstance.

Yes, Baal worship's gone postmodern,
Reckless lies disguised as true . . .
It's the Garden's mass delusion,
And it's really nothing new.

Still, once more we've fallen for it . . .
Same ol', same ol', as they say.
It's the Sin that loves the darkness . . .
Satan whispers: "Let us prey . . ."

————

Lord, we know there is a remnant
That is clinging still to You . . .
Meek and mourning, poor in spirit,
Holding on to what is True.

Father, give us Grace to find You,
Give us Grace to see we're lost . . .
Stir the spirit, Lord, within us.
Take us, please, back to the Cross.

TECHNO-SLABS OF BEEF IN ACTION

Determinism is the philosophical theory that all events, including moral choices, are completely determined by previously existing causes. Determinism is at times understood to preclude free will and claims that essentially humans cannot act otherwise than they do. In other words, "It's Not My Fault-ism."

Prominent biologist and atheist Dr. Jerry Coyne, at the University of Chicago, apparently agrees. In an article titled "Why you really don't have free will" published in *USA Today*, he states that "our brains are simply meat computers that, like real computers, are programmed by our genes and experiences to convert an array of inputs into a predetermined output."[1]

And so, there you have it. According to the popular, contemporary paradigm of atheist-driven "science," human beings are simply preprogrammed machines destined to think, do, and feel whatever the chemicals in the brain mindlessly dictate. Like prearranged dominoes nudged to collapse against each other, our actions, our thoughts, our whims, and our very lives simply run their course *as though* true meaning, transcendent purpose, and free will exist—when, of course, none of them actually exists at all.

Several years ago, the philosopher James Barham made this observation:

> The materialist and reductionist vision of the world favored by consistent Darwinists—what I have been calling "value" or "normative" nihilism—is gaining ground with the public at an alarming rate. If it isn't effectively challenged, our very humanity may be at risk.[2]

———

Son, you're just a meat computer . . .
Nothing more and nothing less;
Every thought you have is programmed.
Don't resist it, just confess!

Input, output . . . prearrangements!
"Jerry-rigged" (to Coyne a phrase),
Robo-man without a purpose,
Scientism's latest craze!

You've no choice . . . You're just a robot,
Neural Dendrite Meat Machine!
All you do is predetermined . . .
Set in motion by your genes.

Spokes 'n' gears, synaptic motors,
There's no "freedom" here to see.
There's no point and no real "reason."
Nihilist futility.

Techno Slabs of Beef in action,
Accidentally comprised!
Pointless, proud, and still progressing . . .
Good and Evil? . . . Neutralized!

Virtue taken off the table . . .
We evolved right past it all!
Truth and Justice? . . . Just illusion.
Empty Shells and standing tall!

Bottom line? . . . You couldn't help it.
Moral conscience fades away . . .
Right and wrong reduced to theory.
Guilt is gone . . . No hell to pay!

ODE TO MR. NYE-GUY

I'm insignificant. . . . I am just another speck of sand.
And the earth really in the cosmic scheme of things is
another speck. And the sun an unremarkable star. . . .
And the galaxy is a speck. I'm a speck on a speck orbiting
a speck among other specks among still other specks in
the middle of specklessness. . . . I suck!¹ —BILL NYE, "THE
SCIENCE GUY"

———————

We're the ones who teach your children,
We're the ones who know what's best.
We're the ones who've been Enlightened
By the Darkness we confess.

We're the ones who swear by Nothing,
Because Nothing's where it's at!
Nothing Nowhere's where we came from . . .
Just like rabbits from a hat!

We're the folks awash in wisdom,
Nihilism is our game,
Scientism's Speck-u-lators . . .
Aren't you glad now that we came . . . ?!

I suck, you suck . . . Cosmic Brothers!
(Idol Humanism's scam.)
Who's the Source of all this Knowledge?
Look no further, son, . . . I am!

Specks of Nye-hilistic nonsense . . .
Just the latest game we play.
Mr. Bill, you see, hath spoken.
Nothing Nowhere's here to stay.

Scientism's new Black Magic,
Walks out onto Center Stage . . .
Prest-O, Change-O . . . There you have it!
Nye-hilism's now uncaged!

———————

"But they won't get away with this for long. Someday
everyone will recognize what fools they are . . ." (2 TIM-
OTHY 3:9 NLT)

THAT'S THE BEST THAT WE CAN DO

"The logical conclusion of relativism is absurdity. Nonsense. A worldview that undermines its own premises."[1] —ERIC METAXAS

"Good" is relative . . . (we're certain).
Good's just goin' with the flow.
You see, "virtue" keeps evolving
That's the latest truth we know.

That's the word we got from Darwin.
Now we're sharing it with you.
Good might just as well be evil.
That's the "best" that we can do.

Darwin begat B. F. Skinner
In a pointless, mindless maze.
Skinner begat Peter Singer,
Who begat these hazy grays.

Now "on purpose" has no meaning
Since we know there's no "design."
There's no Reason, . . . THAT we're sure of!
Really, Real is ill-defined.

In these multi-universes,
There's no telling right from wrong.
What's that hissing in the garden?
Satan's singing right along.

That's the Fate that we've come up with . . .
You might say, "The final Word."
It's the non-sense we're embracing,
In the Land of the Absurd.

Good's a fluctuating premise,
Like a house that's built on sand.
Thou shalt therefore do whatever . . .
Scientism's Tenth Command.

DRAWN AND QUARTERED BY THE STORM

This is what the LORD says:

> "What did your ancestors find wrong with me
>   that led them to stray so far from me?
> They worshiped worthless idols,
>   only to become worthless themselves."
>
> (JEREMIAH 2:5 NLT)

—————

When fallen man, oblivious to his own idolatrous nature, proudly places himself in the position as the arbiter of truth, there is danger at the door. When spinning clumps of clay begin to dictate the rules of engagement to the Potter at the wheel, the outcome is never good. And yet, autonomous man persists in his vainglorious and foolish ways. The problem is nothing new.

In the middle of the eighth century BC, God, through the prophet Hosea, addressed the golden calf idolatries and spiritual rebellion of the northern kingdom of Israel (i.e., Samaria) this way:

> "O Samaria, I reject this calf—this idol you have made. My fury burns against you. How long will it be before one honest man is found among you? When will you admit this calf you worship was made by human hands! It is not God! Therefore, it must be smashed to bits.
>
> "They have sown the wind, and they will reap the whirlwind" (HOSEA 8:5–7A TLB).

In the final analysis, the various idolatries of humanism are a prescription for disaster. Humanism is a philosophy predicated upon earthbound, worldly assumptions arrived at without the warrant and wisdom of divine revelation. It is an ill-conceived house of cards, an edifice with no foundation that is destined to collapse, and then, like chaff, to be blown away in the temporal whirlwinds of history.

———

We esteem our Humanism!
It's the best cure that we've got . . .
Long ago we thought that God was,
But today we think God's not.

We discovered that *true* goodness
Lies quite deep within us all.
We're profoundly proud to tell you
That there never was a "fall."

Those "commandments"? . . . We debunked 'em . . .
Mass confusion's now the norm,
We're now drawn by Nietzsche's Nature,
We'll be quartered by the storm.

As we Babylon in darkness,
And we set our Selves on high,
We are making *awesome* progress . . .
Lifted up, Self-justified.

———

It's the game the devil's playing,
His dead end is near complete.
It's his favorite plan of action . . .
Like a riot in the street.

It's the tempest orchestrated
By the vanities we own.
It's the earthbound whirlwind blowing
Since the lie was Satan-sown.

Revelation's now rejected.
Self-fulfillment is the norm.
We're more drawn to narcissism.
We'll be quartered by the storm.

———————

It is in vain, O men, that you seek within yourselves the cure of all your miseries. All your insight only leads you to the knowledge that it is not in yourselves that you will discover the true and the good . . . Your principal maladies are pride, which cuts you off from God, and sensuality, which binds you to the earth.[1] —Blaise Pascal

———————

Mock on, mock on, Voltaire, Rousseau!
Mock on, Mock on—'Tis all in vain!
You throw the sand against the wind,
and the wind blows it back again.[2]

ABOVE THE MORAL FRAY

... [O]ne of the most entrenched assumptions of moral relativism in our society today: that there is such a thing as morally neutral ground, a place where no judgments are made and where no one seeks to push his personal views on another; where, instead, everyone takes a neutral posture towards the moral convictions of others. This is the essence of tolerance, or so the argument goes.[1]

—GREG KOUKL

———

Don't you see? . . . We're being neutral
When we say "Thou shalt not say!"
We're not really passing judgment . . .
We're above that moral fray.

From up here the view is clearer.
Tolerance, you see, is King.
Here Neutrality is sacred . . .
Where we all can do our thing!

Look, it's fair, and fair is moral . . .
That's now what we teach in school.
Therefore, son, don't buck the System . . .
No! . . . Thou Shalt Not Break This Rule!

———

This is what New Neutral looks like.
It's the wider road we've found . . .
It's the map to Always Happy . . .
(And the latest scam in town).

TELL YOURSELF SOMEHOW IT MATTERS

Perhaps man was neither good nor bad, was only a machine in an insensate universe—his courage no more than a reflex to danger, like the automatic jump at the pin-prick. Perhaps there were no virtues, unless jumping at pin-pricks was a virtue, and humanity only a mechanical donkey led on by the iron carrot of love, through the pointless treadmill of reproduction.[1]
—T. H. WHITE, *THE ONCE AND FUTURE KING*

There is no Christian Gospel if history simply unwinds into a meaningless puddle, if the cosmos simply escapes into a cataclysmic black hole, or if the universe finally dies of exhausted energy. Without belief in a biblical eschatology, there is no Christian hope. Without a sense of perfect moral judgment in the end, the human heart is homeless.[2] —ALBERT MOHLER

We, the homeless and bewildered,
Keep pretending it's OK.
There's no Cause, and we're the rebels . . .
In this pointless passion play.

There's no "good" news, there's no "bad" news,
There's just Nothing in the end.
There's no Purpose, there's no Virtue,
No real "meaning" to defend.

It's the Black Hole that we're stuck with,
It's the burden that we bear.
There's no question, there's no answer,
Still, we must pretend to "care."

So, keep lying to yourself, son . . .
(Maybe drugs can pull you through?).
Tell yourself somehow it matters.
Just make up what's true for you.

Gather 'round you endless idols
To alleviate the pain.
Find relief, boy, in your "safe place"
Even though it may be feigned.

———————

On the other hand, young fella,
All may not be doom 'n' gloom.
Take another look, why don't you,
At that Jewish empty tomb.

Who knows? . . . Maybe there's the answer.
Maybe there's the antidote
To the corner we've backed into . . .
(Who knows? . . . Maybe there IS Hope!)

HAVE YOU READ THE NEWS TODAY? . . . OH, BOY

> "Every thing is to be recommended to the public by some sort of synonym which is really a pseudonym. It is a talent that goes with the time of electioneering and advertisement and newspaper headlines; but what ever else such a time may be, it certainly is not specially a time of truth."[1] —G. K. CHESTERTON

Six hundred years before the time of Jesus, Jeremiah, "the weeping prophet," surveyed the spiritual condition of his beloved nation of Judah. He saw an apostate people in spiritual rebellion chasing after false gods. He saw corruption. He saw a proud, self-absorbed, and adulterous nation—a culture in decay.

Jeremiah lived among a people who had "not obeyed the LORD its God or responded to correction," a people from whose lips truth itself had "vanished" (Jeremiah 7:28).

He saw babies being sacrificed in the Valley of Slaughter.[2]

Jeremiah mourned, wept, and warned of God's impending judgment. And, as history proved, judgment did indeed fall, just as the prophet had foreseen.

Jeremiah . . . chapter seven.

Does it sound familiar yet?

Has the Truth been deconstructed?

Do we yawn with no regret?

In the Valley of this Slaughter
Will we turn to see the Light?
Or remain among the ruins
In the "comfort" of this blight?

Son, will Baal keep on applauding?
Will Queen Asherah approve?
Will we listen to correction?
Has God's blessing been removed?

Will we keep on making idols
Made of wood and stone and gold?
Will we disregard the warning
Of the gospel we've been told?

Will we wander in the desert?
Will we mock the Word we heard?
Are the lukewarm waters rising
In this cauldron being stirred?

———————

Red truth, blue truth, green truth, new truth . . .
Let's assess the damage done.
His truth, her truth on the broad way,
Meanwhile, true Truth's on the run.

There's a shadow in this valley . . .
Cast by Molech on the Left.
On the right? . . . My word, it's Mammon!
And the smell, my friend, is death.

Here's a shovel . . . Let's keep digging!
Deeper, darker . . . Take your pick!
Same old grave mistake repeated . . .
Satan's same ol' magik trick.

———————

"The depravity of man is at once the most empirically verifiable reality but at the same time most intellectually resisted fact."[3] —Malcolm Muggeridge

Lukewarm Water Doldrums

"I know all the things you do,

that you are neither hot nor cold.

I wish that you were one or the other!

But since you are like lukewarm water,

neither hot nor cold,

I will spit you out of my mouth!"

(Revelation 3:15–16 NLT)

CRUISE THE NEO-PAGAN WATERS

"That which begins with shamefacedness, equivocation, hesitation, and compromise will ripen into apostasy."[1] —CHARLES SPURGEON

"We're moments away. I think the culture is already there. And the church will continue to be even more irrelevant when it quotes letters from 2,000 years ago as their best defense."[2] —ROB BELL

————

Rob Bell climbs into the crow's nest,
First Mate Oprah gazes east,
Goddess Gaia's in the galley
Stirring up a New Age Feast.

Cruise the Neo-Pagan waters . . .
Just be happy! Have your way!
Yep, it's time to do your own thing! . . .
Test the winds! . . . It's A-OK!

On the good ship SS Tol'rance
Captained by the Inner Child . . .
Quite unmoored from Truth and Virtue
Set adrift . . . mile after mile.

Navigation by "good feelings"
Sailing where we darn well please,
Sunning on the Deck of Pleasures,
Basking in hypocrisies.

We've abandoned map 'n' sextant,
Winds of Change we're trusting now . . .
Yes, my friend, we're making headway!
(Big Grin, Smiley Face . . . and how!)

Proudly tacking into darkness,
Compass? . . . Hey, man, there's no need!
We're not quite sure where we're going,
But who cares? . . . We're gaining speed!

We're convinced we're making "progress"
Toward just what . . . well, who's to say?
We believe if we keep moving,
Everything will be OK!

No more True North for direction,
We're the Rudderless 'n' Proud . . .
Sailing out here East of Eden
While remaining still unbowed.

In this Current Liberalism
There's no Anchor yet in sight,
We can't fathom Good or Evil . . .
No, my friend, no wrong or right.

Sailing blind into the Fog Bank
Of the Vague, Unsure, and Blurred . . .
Trusting in our Wishful Thinking . . .
Tossing overboard God's Word.

Aimless drift in lukewarm water,
Spirit Doldrums take their toll . . .
Yes, the issue's quite Titanic,
While the Gospel's left untold.

Hoist the Sail of Good Intentions!
Disregard those rocky straits! . . .
On this Ocean of Deception,
Satan smirks . . . (and simply waits).

———————

Father, thank you for the Anchor,
Thank You for that precious Gift! . . .
Thank You for this Faith born in us,
Help your children still adrift.

———————

In the presence of God and of Christ Jesus, who will judge the living and the dead, and in view of his appearing and his kingdom, I give you this charge: Preach the word; be prepared in season and out of season; correct, rebuke and encourage—with great patience and careful instruction. (2 TIMOTHY 4:1–2)

"He must hold firmly to the trustworthy message as it has been taught, so that he can encourage others by sound doctrine and refute those who oppose it." (TITUS 1:9)

PILGRIMS OF POSTMODERN PREACHING

"Much of the church is either asleep or in bed with the world."[1] —DOUGLAS GROOTHUIS

We have faith that truth's illusion . . .
And it can't set prisoners free.
We're more taken with the world now . . .
Since it loves both you and me.

We've arranged for our acquittal . . .
Redetermined all the facts.
We've dismissed "sin" as the problem . . .
Wiped it out, to be exact.

We've devised another gospel
For the kids in Sunday School.
There's no longer need for mourning.
We've decided lukewarm's cool.

With an emphasis on "Doubtful,"
We're promoting "Feeling Fine."
We've declared God therapeutic,
Precious few would say "divine."

We have vetoed condemnation.
It's just mercy we deserve.
Justice? . . . Up for arbitration.
We grade "Holy" on the curve.

We're postmodern pilgrim preachers,
"Truth," *per se*, we've put to bed . . .
Some have tried to resurrect it.
We, however, think it's dead.

FAITH IN FAITH REMOVES ALL DOUBT

> Faith is not an instinct. It certainly is not a feeling—
> feelings don't help much when you're in the lions' den
> or hanging on a wooden Cross. Faith is not inferred
> from the happy way things work. It is an act of will, a
> choice, based on the unbreakable Word of a God who
> cannot lie, and who showed us what love and obedi-
> ence and sacrifice mean, in the person of Jesus Christ.[1]
> —ELISABETH ELLIOT

Do you sometimes hear folks say, "Oh, yes, I have faith!"?

When you hear that, do you then wait . . . (with bated breath) . . . for what, if anything, might come next? Do you lean forward in pregnant anticipation and think to yourself . . . (*Yes? . . . AND . . . ?*)? Do you think to yourself *Is there an object of this "faith" that you profess to have, or is this simply a "feeling" . . . an open-ended statement of generic wishful thinking?*

Is this some sort of instinct? Something akin to having faith in faith?

Faith, we're sure, is all that matters . . .
Faith is what it's all about.
Faith in WHAT's not that important.
Faith in faith removes all doubt.

Is this faith like crossing fingers?
Faith in Drudge? . . . In CBS?
Faith in all our very good deeds?
Faith that we've all passed the test?

Is this faith in Mother Nature
And in scientific facts?
Faith in all our good intentions . . .
Faith in faith keeps us on track.

Faith in even Bigger Brothers . . .
(Whether green or red or blue?)
Faith in Guns . . . (or maybe Roses)?
Peace 'n' Love? . . . Whatever's new?

Faith in mammon making headway?
Faith in averaging the Dow?
Faith in tea leaves? . . . Faith in crystals?
Faith in living in the now?

Faith in faith's the Magic Bullet.
(Isn't that what Jesus said?)
"Saved by faith" sincerely felt, sir,
Is the faith that's in our head.

Yes, *sincerity* is key here.
It's the only key we need.
It's the way we get to heaven.
We have faith it's guaranteed.

Faith in honest speculation
Is enough to get us in.
Even faith in nothing really
Should be good enough, my friend.

We have faith the gods are righteous,
(And what's right is what WE say!)
We have faith that when we voted
Righteousness was on display.

Faith in "goodness" is a safe bet.
Faith in progress is as well.
That's the gospel we believe in.
Keep the faith: there is no hell.

———

Give us faith, Lord, in the gospel . . .
In the Word that You revealed!
Give us grace to hear it clearly,
By your Spirit, seal the deal.

Give us faith to know the Truth, Lord.
Give us grace to comprehend.
Take us to the Cross of Calv'ry,
Please, before we reach the end.

———

"So then faith *comes* by hearing, and hearing by the word of God." (ROMANS 10:17 NKJV)

IT'S ANOTHER ICE CREAM SUNDAY

It's another Ice Cream Sunday,
Double scoops, we long to hear,
Sweet 'n' gooey grand distractions,
Happy thoughts for itching ears.

Tasty sugar-coated sermons,
Just the latest gospel fudged.
Sweet, sweet nothings from the pulpit
'Bout a God-Who'd-Never-Judge!

Keep those compromises coming . . .
Just like sprinkles . . . pour 'em on!
Nuts and multi-colored gummies
'Til the Gospel Truth is gone.

You can pick your favorite flavors,
And may do so liberally!
You can blend 'em all together . . .
No one here will disagree!

Choose among your favorite toppings.
Come on in and have a seat!
Top it all off with a cherry
Just to make your joy complete!

LURE 'EM IN WITH SWEET CONCOCTIONS

> If we say that we have no sin, we are deceiving our-
> selves and the truth is not in us. If we confess our sins,
> He is faithful and righteous to forgive us our sins and
> to cleanse us from all unrighteousness. If we say that
> we have not sinned, we make Him a liar and His word
> is not in us. (1 JOHN 1:8–10 NASB)

———

The "Good News" of the Bible, by necessity and design, begins with the very real *bad news* of universal condemnation (see Ezekiel 18:4; John 3:18; Romans 3:1–20, etc.). We all stand guilty before God's standard of holiness. No exceptions and no wiggle room.

Without the clear understanding of the truth and the reality of sin and its deadly eternal consequences (the very bad news), the much esteemed *good news* becomes inconsequential—in essence, a watered down scenario that is reduced to "no news" at all.

Nevertheless, today we see professing Christians, liberal schol-ars, and theologians removing the bad news from the gospel equa-tion altogether. By doing so, they mistakenly assume they are doing their listeners a favor. After all, who in their right mind wants to be the bearer of bad news? (Nobody likes that!) And so they kick against the goads, rationalize, and tell themselves:

"Let's just skip *that* part . . . (what the Bible calls "the curse") . . . and get right to the blessing, the 'Jesus loves me, this I know . . .'" message. We certainly don't want to frighten anyone's inner child or cause any spiritual discomfort. After all, we want to be popular, and besides, causing folks to be uncomfortable just wouldn't be nice."

And so, the "No news is good news" gospel message is broadcast far and wide, and everybody feels just fine. The way things ought to be. The feel-good, "just be nice" message of wishful thinking and good intentions soothingly resonates all around . . . like a lullaby, a scented candle, a box of chocolates, or a bubble bath.

The emerging false gospel of "Let-Us-Tell-You-What-You-Want-to-Hear" (first introduced in the Garden of Eden[1]) is alive and very much in vogue today within much of affluent Christendom.

Toothless; truthless; and ultimately, ruthless . . . Ear-Tickling 101.[2] We have been warned:

> For the time will come when they will not endure sound doctrine; but *wanting* to have their ears tickled, they will accumulate for themselves teachers in accordance to their own desires, and will turn away their ears from the truth and will turn aside to myths. (2 TIMOTHY 4:3–4 NASB)

There's no need for confrontation . . .
Stroke 'em, soothe 'em, make 'em smile!
That's the way to grow a church now;
Don't offend the inner child!

Lure 'em in with sweet concoctions,
Tell 'em what they want to hear!
Help them understand *true* wisdom:
God's NOT something you should fear!

Help 'em see they're not so bad now,
Help 'em know sin's no big deal,
Help 'em see that shame's not healthy . . .
And their guilt's not really real.

Help 'em know the "curse" is fiction
And "The Fall" just never was.
Get them past that "judgment" nonsense . . .
Why? You ask? . . . Well, just because!

Help 'em see God's *only* Mercy . . .
(Disregard the "Holy" stuff).
Hammer home that good intentions
Are what makes 'em "good enough"!

Pump 'em up with words like "Glory!"
Help 'em see The Way is wide!
Teach 'em Self-improvement lessons . . .
And that Jesus may have lied.

Lord, we know your Word's unwelcome
To the ear of dying man . . .
It's all nonsense to his reason,
And he just won't understand.

Such is mankind in denial . . .
Sin's unreason on display . . .
Lord, have mercy, please, upon us!
Teach us why You came, we pray!

By your Spirit, grant discernment,
Seal in us true Life and Light . . .
Help us then see Sin within us;
Lord, reveal our deadly plight

Father God, then please forgive us . . .
Show us why Christ came to die.
Grant to us true revelation:
Show us Jesus crucified.

———————

"The person without the Spirit does not accept the things that come from the Spirit of God but considers them foolishness, and cannot understand them because they are discerned only through the Spirit."
(1 CORINTHIANS 2:14)

THERAPEUTIC PUPPY DOGMA

In far too many churches today, biblical teaching has been reduced to its lowest common denominator. We have been taught and continue to teach what some have called moralistic therapeutic deism, which when reduced to its bare essential is little more than a philosophy of being nice at any cost. Sadly, we are passing this "religious" system down to our children. We have rushed past the Scriptures, cherry-picking a few thoughts and verses here and there that seem to fit the latest contemporary social agenda, and then we hurry on. It is all very self-satisfying—and that, of course, is the point. One author has written that

> American young people are devotees of non-judgmental openness, self-determination, and the authority of personal experience. Religion stays in the background of their lives, where God watches over them without making demands of them. God, above all else, is 'nice.'[1]

Author James D. Conley has explained the concept in this way:

> The dogma of Moralistic Therapeutic Deism is this: God exists, and desires that people are good, nice, and fair to one another. God can be called upon to assure happiness and to resolve crises. Being good, nice, and fair assures eternal salvation in heaven.[2]

Welcome to our Puppy Dogma,
Quite the soft and cuddly sight,
Waggy-taily, always friendly . . .
And this Dogma doesn't bite!

Here's religion we can hang with,
Here's a good God to enjoy!
Puppy Dogma co-existing,
Quite laid back . . . a real good boy!

If you want, he'll just roll over,
Or he'll fetch and play all day!
Guaranteed to keep you happy
In a pluralistic way.

He can "Stay!" right where you want him,
Or he might just tag along!
He will never be judgmental
In the face of right or wrong!

When you're down, he'll lift your spirits.
When you're low, he'll get you high.
Therapeutic Puppy Dogma,
True blue, trusty, *semper fi.*

Bottom line, he's reassuring.
He'll make sure you're feeling good!
He'll come running when you whistle . . .
Like good Puppy Dogmas should!

MAKE A WISH FOR HEAVEN'S SAKE

Beware of manufacturing a God of your own: a God who is all mercy, but not just; a God who is all love, but not holy; a God who has a heaven for everybody, but a hell for none; a God who can allow good and bad to exist side by side on earth, and will make no distinction between good and bad in eternity. Such a God is an idol of your own creation as real as Jupiter or Moloch; as true an idol as any snake or crocodile in an Egyptian temple; as true an idol as was ever moulded out of brass or clay. The hands of your own notions and emotions have made him. He is not the God of the Bible, and aside the God of the Bible there is no God at all.[1]
—J. C. RYLE

———

Make a good God to your liking,
Shaped and molded as you will . . .
Just divine and just like magic:
"God!" . . . your therapeutic pill.

Look, let's really keep it simple.
Give your mind a needed a break.
Close your eyes and just imagine . . .
Make a wish for heaven's sake.

Find a church that suits your Selfie,
One where you can just be YOU!
One that emphasizes feeling,
One that makes your dreams come true.

Take a deep breath, find your rhythm.
Keep on following your bliss!
Find someone to preach God *your* way.
(Let's keep Scripture out of this!)

Make up your own revelation,
'Til it feels just right to you.
Make God into your own image;
Then do what *you* want to do.

WE SING HYMNS AND HERS

One danger . . . that I'm fairly sure [the apostles] did *not* face was the pressure to be "nice." . . . In our time, we have lived through the expansion of the market, the explosion of media influence, and what Philip Rieff of Chicago University calls "the triumph of the therapeutic." We are immersed in values and visions of the good life, which we inculcate with almost every breath that we breathe. It is a cultural moment where looking good and feeling good are paramount, and anything that threatens, disturbs, or challenges the cultural value-setters is ruled out of court.[1] —STUART MCALLISTER

Are you living out "The Nice Life"?
Have you polished your appeal?
If your answer's "No, not really,"
Have we got a special deal!

"Happy" is our main objective,
Popularity's our aim.
Our Religion's free 'n' easy,
Thus avoiding guilt and shame.

We have re-imagined "holy"
And we've sugar-coated "grace;"
We sing hymns and hers (for balance)
To please everybody's taste.

Yes, we're here to stroke your ego.
We've moved past commands and laws.
We think maybe God's a process
With no bottom lines to draw.

We do doctrine open-minded,
And we don't do creeds at all.
We're quite proud of all our progress,
And we look down on "The Fall."

We're the Church of Most Attractive . . .
Compromise is what we do.
It's not difficult at all, sir,
Once you've deconstructed "true."

Now that truth's been proven errant . . .
Frankly, sir, we think it's best . . .
We've been told by higher critics
We should give "the truth" a rest.

Smiley faces on our bumpers.
"Just be nice!" is what we preach.
We've got fables on our tables . . .
Happy days within our reach!

———————

"In those days . . . everyone did as they saw fit." (JUDGES 21:25)

"The way of a fool is right in his own eyes: but he that hearkeneth unto counsel is wise." (PROVERBS 12:15 KJV)

You're going to find that there will be times when people will have no stomach for solid teaching, but will fill up on spiritual junk food—catchy opinions that tickle their fancy. They'll turn their backs on truth and chase mirages. But *you*—keep your eye on what you're doing; accept the hard times along with the good; keep the Message alive; do a thorough job as God's servant. (2 TIMOTHY 4:3–5 MSG)

IT'S THE ZEITGEIST THAT WE'RE INTO

During the late nineteenth century, German theologians and philosophers began the process of biblical "higher criticism." They engaged in the hard work of examining and dismantling the Scriptures in the light of advancing "science" and scientific inquiry. The dual notions of divine revelation and the "miraculous" were put under the microscope of enlightened pragmatism and progressive human reason and were found sorely lacking. The higher critics sauntered onto the center stage of modern history and proudly took a bow.

It was a field day for the skeptics.

Friedrich Nietzsche saw the writing on the wall. In 1882 he wrote *The Gay Science*. In it he introduced the prophetic madman—a supposed fool who wandered through the public square:

> The madman jumped into their midst and pierced them with his eyes. "Whither is God?" he cried; "I will tell you. *We have killed him*—you and I. All of us are his murderers. But how did we do this? How could we drink up the sea? Who gave us the sponge to wipe away the entire horizon?[1]

We took the higher critics' bait. We have taken the sponge they handed off to us and have dutifully followed in their footsteps, until today the fog of religious humanism and the reign of nihilistic postmodernist thought has nearly blotted out the light of truth. We have sown the wind, and today we are reaping the consequences.

———

Now that Zarathustra's speaking
To the world so loud and clear,
We're enthralled by Nothing really . . .
Nietzsche now has gained our ear.

God is dead . . . Yes, dead and buried,
And it's time you saw the light.
We've got new truth for creating . . .
Hidden truth still out of sight.

Deconstruction in the meantime
Is the realm we're playing in.
So remove those old foundations.
(Start with all that talk of "sin.")

Re-imagine every Plumb Line.
Take away those Ten Commands!
Start from scratch here in the darkness.
Raise the roof-beam, Super-Man!

We must overcome tradition,
Wipe away horizon lines.
Justice must be readjusted.
"Good" brought down and redefined.

Ancient creeds hold no more promise.
We need yet a Better One.
We must re-invent The Story . . .
We've arrived to get it done!

———

It's the *zeitgeist* that we're into.
Pagan principles restored!
Grab your pitchforks, light your torches . . .
We're the ones we've waited for!

———————

"Christendom has had a series of revolutions and in each one of them Christianity has died. Christianity has died many times and risen again; for it had a God who knew the way out of the grave."[2] —G. K. CHESTERTON

NOW THE GOSPEL'S MOSTLY NICE

The aim in marketing is to stimulate, excite, and satisfy the consumer. Madison Avenue church marketing strategies and techniques have been in full swing for several decades now. Individual churches and even entire denominations have enthusiastically taken the promotional plunge. But if we survey the moral landscape of America today (and if we're honest), we must admit that the Mad Men church campaign has not exactly helped to improve the moral or spiritual health of Western culture. In fact, one might be tempted to suggest that just the opposite is true. As A. W. Tozer once remarked, "A church fed on excitement is no new testament church at all. The desire for surface stimulation is a sure mark of the fallen nature, the very thing Christ died to deliver us from."[1]

————

Yes, the Mad Men road to glory
Is the broad way that we're on.
Glam-I Am is now our theme psalm,
While the wrath of God is gone.

The seduction, though, is friendly.
And the sales pitch *does* entice.
The temptation's been successful . . .
Now the gospel's simply "nice."

You'll be comfortable inside, sir.
Here we'll set your mind at ease.
All our pews have been refurbished.
We're quite certain you'll be pleased!

We've got music for all ages . . .
Great big screens . . . All digitized!
Cafe latte in the narthex.
Fundamentals? . . . Compromised.

We've got programs for the children,
K through 12 and room for more!
Clowns with puppets roam the classrooms.
Fun for all goes door to door.

We won't mention "condemnation."
Sin is off the table, too.
Words like that aren't very helpful,
Here that's just not what we do.

By de-emphasizing Sinai
And downplaying Calvary,
We've discovered extra profits
And increased prosperity.

Satisfaction's what we offer.
Yes, excitement's in the air!
Here the word we preach is upbeat,
And God knows we really care.

We've got droves of happy people
Who would love to say "Hello!"
Folks who have it all together . . .
Really great folks you should know.

Yes, we think you'll fit right in here.
And to *that* we'll testify!
We'd be proud as punch to have you.
You seem like our kind of guy!

––––––––––

Marketing savvy demands that the offense of the cross must be downplayed, salesmanship requires that negative subjects like divine wrath must be avoided. Consumer satisfaction means that the standard of righteousness cannot be raised too high. . . . [T]he market-driven ministry philosophy appeals to the very worst mood in our age. It caters to people whose first love is self and who do not care for God unless they can have Him without disrupting their selfish lifestyles. Promise such people a religion that will allow them to be comfortable in their materialism and comfortable in their self-love and they will respond in droves.[2]
—JOHN MACARTHUR

ONCE WE EVEN USED THE MAP

The author, theologian, and noted Christian apologist Douglas Groothuis recently observed:

> America is adrift—morally, politically, and spiritually. The anchor broke off and sank to the bottom of the ocean. The rudder rusted out and fell down to the bottom as well. Its garish sails—festooned with mindless slogans—take it wherever the wild gusts of wind blow it. Few stand against the wind. But some must—not for the sake of being different or authentic, but because of the uncompromising insistence of the truth.[1]

Author and theologian Sinclair Ferguson has noted that apostasy grows as an "indifference to the way of the Cross, a drifting that is not reversed by the knowledge of biblical warning."[2]

The foundations of Western civilization are quaking today. The decades long secular onslaught has taken its toll, not just in the public square but, more tragically, also within the traditional church community. Many of the fundamental doctrines of the faith have been downloaded into the murky and briny deep of postmodernist thinking. The gospel truth has been declared by some to be a stultifying encumbrance to the itching ears of a pre-programmed and digitized generation. After all, who's got the time to think and listen today? We would much rather splash around in the lukewarm shallows of easy-believism and feel-good, compromised preaching and teaching.

We have tried to scuttle theological Old Ironsides and re-imagine for ourselves a toy tugboat for the tub.

———

We set sail on Easy-Breezies,
Then we scuttled all the rules.
We're in dark, uncharted waters.
Welcome to the Ship of Fools.

Raise that Skull 'n' Crossbones Banner!
Jettison God's Moral Laws.
Cast off scripture, creeds and doctrine.
Out here fishin' for applause.

Captain Ahab's loyal crewmen,
Idol-chasing buccaneers.
Waterlogged, a bit unsteady,
Rebels with no God to fear.

At one time we used the Compass,
But we tossed it overboard.
Once we sought and found the North Star,
But today it's just ignored.

Once we had a map to go by
As we sailed the briny deep.
Once we utilized the Anchor.
Once we had a course to keep!

No more need for maps or rudders . . .
Who needs Anchors anyway!?
We're all ship-shape Jolly Rogers
Boastful brigands . . . come what may.

"Land Ho!" must be out there somewhere.
Then again, we might be wrong.
We've set sail into the darkness
Where we *feel* our way along.

We've been gazing at our naval,
Drifting out here aimlessly.
We're quite proud of our direction . . .
Sailing these Aposta-Seas.

We've consulted "higher critics."
That was our first big mistake.
Now we're trawling for direction
In our own misguided wake.

We've bailed out the Living Water,
Now we're drifting toward the shoals.
We can't fathom why we're sinking.
(No one sees the gaping holes.)

Stern to bow, it looks like trouble.
Lukewarm water's rushing in.
We preached Nice 'n' Easy-Pleasey.
Now we're lost at sea again.

FLASHES IN THE PAN

The Welsh Protestant minister David Martyn Lloyd-Jones once observed that "when the church is absolutely different from the world, she invariably attracts it. It is then that the world is made to listen to her message, though it may hate it at first."[1]

Too often today this advice is ignored, or, worse, even flipped on its head. The church, in an effort to be found acceptable by the world (and not at first hated and disdained), has endeavored to become just like the culture it has been called to reach and to redeem. By trying to cater to the world's fanciful whims and Hollywood ways, the church has forfeited her sharply distinctive, countercultural message. By trying to be like the latest thing, her message eventually goes the way of all those other "latest things" that have come and gone. By trying to reach the world by being *like* the world, her voice becomes just one more muffled sales pitch lost in the shuffle of an already oversaturated marketplace of secular philosophies, ideas, trends, and mundane fads—dull and boring. The strategy of accommodation may appeal for a moment; indeed, it may briefly "flash in the pan."

But all that glitters is not gold.

———

Look, with all these bells and whistles,
Flashing lights that entertain.
Never ending plans and programs . . .
Who needs talk of crimson stain?

This theatrical arrangement
Seems to really draw them in.
Let's not blow it Sunday morning . . .
Preacher, please, don't mention sin.

Let's just concentrate on "happy"
From these massive movie screens.
And for extra soulful measure
Mystic mist from smoke machines.

Let's just keep it all attractive.
Let's not preach 'em all away!
Let's promote self-satisfaction,
Here and now . . . and *every* day!

Just don't mention "condemnation."
Put "Christ crucified" on hold.
Zero in on "social justice."
That's the key . . . (or so I'm told).

———————

"I do not think it is a harsh judgment to say that the most obvious feature of the life of the Christian church today is, alas, superficiality."[2] —MARTYN LLOYD-JONES

THE GOD WE'RE NOW DIVINING

Every Christmas season we are confronted with a version of the advent of Jesus so perversely processed through a consumer-oriented blender and stripped of spiritual meaning that the Bible-believing Christian must cringe with incredulity. We are presented annually with the mammon-made Messiah, represented by Santa, his jovial helper, who waves good wishes at the rear end of a thousand downtown parades. Sadly, such a perverted picture of God is re-enforced by far too many churches every Sunday. As theologian and author Ulrich Lehner has put it,

> [This] "Santa God" gives us a warm, fuzzy feeling—like a cozy blanket on a cold winter day—and brings us what we want. This God is the ultimate vending machine: As long as you are "nice" here and there, you get a present and perhaps even a place in heaven.[1]

———

He's the God of lovey-dovies,
He's the feel-good God we've got.
Like a Teddy Bear or blanket,
He's the God we like a lot!

He's the comfy God we're craving,
He's the God of wishing wells.
He's the God of good intentions
And the God who *really* sells!

He's the God who only pleases,
He's the God who's never "mean."
He's the smiley God of rainbows
Here to boost our self-esteem.

He's the God who stuffs our stockings.
He's the God who hands out toys.
He's the God of cotton candy
Who obeys the girls and boys.

He's the God of jolly laughter,
Dream-time sugar plums and more!
He's the God we're now divining.
That's the God we're pulling for.

HE'S THE ROBIN HOOD WE NEED!

Barabbas's name appears as *bar-Abbas* in the Greek texts of the Gospels. It is derived ultimately from the Aramaic אבא-רב, Bar-abbâ, "son of the father."

———

We would rather have bar-Abbas . . .
He's the one who must be freed!
Let's rev up the insurrection . . .
He's the Robin Hood we need!

He's bar-Abbas (Rebel Leader),
He's the father's son[1] we'll save!
We're Pro-Choice, and so we're choosing
To keep this one from the grave.

Mr. Pilate, make it happen!
We're the crowd you need to please.
Wash your hands! . . . Come on! Just do it!
Every Pharisee agrees!

———

Do we champion bar-Abbas?
Is the multitude still stirred?
Are our hearts bound in rebellion?
Do we yell amongst the herd?

———

Now at the feast he used to release for them one prisoner for whom they asked. And among the rebels in prison, who had committed murder in the insurrection, there was a man called Barabbas. And the crowd came up and began to ask Pilate to do as he usually did for them. And he answered them, saying, "Do you want me to release for you the King of the Jews?" For he perceived that it was out of envy that the chief priests had delivered him up. But the chief priests stirred up the crowd to have him release for them Barabbas instead. And Pilate again said to them, "Then what shall I do with the man you call the King of the Jews?" And they cried out again, "Crucify him." And Pilate said to them, "Why? What evil has he done?" But they shouted all the more, "Crucify him." So Pilate, wishing to satisfy the crowd, released for them Barabbas, and having scourged Jesus, he delivered him to be crucified. (MARK 15:6–15 ESV)

FAITH IN PHARAOH'S BORN AGAIN

It has been several decades now since jurist Robert Bork wrote, "The rough beast of decadence, a long time in gestation, having reached its maturity in the last three decades, now sends us slouching towards our new home, not Bethlehem but Gomorrah."[1]

The rough beast of decadence that Bork referred to has since become a ravenous, multi-headed monster, a metastasizing hydra that has spread its poisonous and paralyzing venom into every conceivable nook and cranny of Judeo-Christian civilization.

———————

Friend, we slouched right past Gomorrah . . .
It's the tale that never fails.
Since we deca-danced 'round Sinai,
We're in bedlam now with Baal.

We're progressing back to Egypt.
Faith in Pharaoh's born again!
Sabbath resting in Big Brother,
Where there's no such thing as sin.

We turned back from Canaan's promise.
Never mind that House of Bread.
Where's the meat? The leeks and onions?
(Stuff we're lusting for instead.)

———————

Satisfaction's the attraction
When there is no God to fear.
Hedonism is the "come on"
In the Land of Itching Ears.

———

Then the foreign rabble who were traveling with the Israelites began to crave the good things of Egypt. And the people of Israel also began to complain. "Oh, for some meat!" they exclaimed. "We remember the fish we used to eat for free in Egypt. And we had all the cucumbers, melons, leeks, onions, and garlic we wanted. But now our appetites are gone. All we ever see is this manna!" (NUMBERS 11:4–6 NLT)

CARE BEAR GOD

"We have very efficiently pared the claws of the Lion of Judah, certified him 'meek and mild,' and recommended him as a fitting household pet for pale curates and pious old ladies."[1] —DOROTHY SAYERS

"Christianity minus intelligible doctrine is simply unintelligible doctrine minus Christianity."[2] —GORDON CLARK, PHILOSOPHER/THEOLOGIAN

Approximately one hundred years ago, Princeton University theology professor B. B. Warfield observed that "an anemic Christianity that is not virile enough to strive for truth can never possess the nerve to die for it. A truth not worth defending very soon becomes a truth not worth professing."[3]

In his day, Warfield recognized a gospel that was fast becoming merely "a form of godliness" (see 2 Timothy 3:5), an anemic and toothless false gospel that had been marinating in the speculative juices of nineteenth-century higher criticism. He recognized the signs of an emerging and increasingly impotent church that was abandoning the solid ground of truth (the "faith of her fathers") and was beginning to sink into the quicksand of a watered down, pluralistic form of spiritual universalism and moral relativism—a church that would eventually proclaim that ALL religions and belief systems are speculative at best.

A hundred years ago, Warfield could see the writing on the wall, and his ominous and prescient admonition has come to fruition. Today, that writing on the wall has become a sprawling, scrawling hodge-podge of indecipherable theological graffiti. And while it may be appealing and attractive to most, it certainly is not the radical and revolutionary Word of Truth revealed through the Holy Spirit-inspired prophets and apostles . . . and in Jesus Christ, the incarnate Word.

Throughout recorded history, sinful, idolatrous man has desired a pantheon of comfortable, custom-made "gods." Sadly, today's contemporary church seems more than willing to provide for those longed for "felt needs."

Today's radically liberalized church seems more than willing to present herself to a jaded . . . and dying . . . Western civilization as little more than just another entertainment option to be considered, a "worship experience" guaranteed not to offend . . . a friendly, hard-working institution that aims to please. The contemporary "Church of Best Wishes" stands in the audition line, desperately trying to make herself appealing and attractive to the itching ears of an emotion-driven world already numbed and bored by the false hope of gimmickry and gadgets and the empty promises of the Cult of Whatever's New.

Too often, the upbeat and fashionable church, liberated as it is from the tedious constraints of doctrine and tradition, has become a perverse mixture of pop-cultural psychotherapeutic banalities and sugarcoated, toothless generalities. And in a fit of deluded irrationality, the Church of the Broad Convenient Way has decided that the only sin there really is is the unforgivable sin of mentioning "sin" at all. The Commandments—now reassessed and officially designated "Outdated!"—have been scrubbed and replaced with a list of nebulous "All You Need is Love"-isms. In too many cases, this "liberated" brand of Christendom has foolishly come to believe that it is better to amuse, mollify, and mimic the world than it is to call broken, repentant sinners out of the world and into the Body of Christ. The current, candy-coated mantra of "Tolerance" and best wishes has superseded the mention of original sin, holy judgment, and the need for repentance. The cross of Christ has become an unmentionable embarrassment to many.

"Just be nice!" has pre-empted "Justice reigns!" The Lion of the Tribe of Judah has been downgraded to the What's-Your-Pleasure Care Bear God of Happy Feelings, . . . Aslan has been unceremoniously demoted to a sweet and lovable Pooh.

————

All religions, sir, are equal—
Yes, our Caring God agrees;
Let there be no condemnation . . .
Drop that "sin"-talk, . . . if you please!

In the end, sin makes no difference;
'Cause our Care Bear God is fair!
And a fair God couldn't bear it,
No, a fair God wouldn't dare.

You can trust us . . . Just be happy!
With a Care Bear God like this,
Take the trespass off the table . . .
Guilt's not on The Care Bear list.

So again, I'll just remind you,
In the end there is no "shame";
No "conviction," "Law," or "Dogma" . . .
Yes, the wrathful God's been tamed!

I reiterate . . . Don't sweat it!
Come, embrace our Care Bear God;
Just enjoy those Fuzzy Feelings—
God is there to give His nod.

Bowing down to all our wishes,
He approves of all our ways!
Yes, He bends to our good pleasures . . .
His commands are Sugar-Glazed.

Yes, the Cotton-Candied Gospel
Satisfies all itching ears!
Never mind those Sinai Tablets
That have plagued us all these years!

———————

Man believes the Word of Skeptics . . .
(It's more comfortable that way!)
Talk of "truth" and "revelation"
Bows to Doubt . . . then fades to gray.

Yes, from here the Cross is foolish,
Shame and guilt and sin? . . . Absurd!
Hell itself has been discarded . . .
We trust in the Neutered Word.

Holy Spirit, give us vision . . .
May thy true Light help us see;
Lord, come chase away this darkness . . .
Show us Truth at Calvary!

———————

That preaching is sadly defective which dwells exclu-
sively on the mercies of God and joys of heaven, and
never sets forth the terrors of the Lord and the miseries of hell. It may be popular, but it is not scriptural; it
may amuse and satisfy, but it will not save.[4] —J. C. RYLE

PREACH IT LAID-BACK, MELLOW, LUKEWARM

Unannounced and mostly undetected there has come in modern times a new cross into popular evangelical circles. It is like the old cross, but different: the likenesses are superficial; the differences, fundamental. . . . The new cross is not opposed to the human race; rather, it is a friendly pal and, if understood aright, it is the source of oceans of good clean fun and innocent enjoyment. It lets Adam live without interference. His life motivation is unchanged; he still lives for his own pleasure. . . . [It] encourages a new and entirely different evangelistic approach. The evangelist . . . preaches not contrasts but similarities. He seeks to key into public interest by showing that Christianity makes no unpleasant demands; rather, it offers the same thing the world does, only on a higher level. . . . [I]t redirects him. It gears him into a cleaner and jollier way of living and saves his self-respect.[1] —A. W. TOZER

———

Preach it, brother! Make 'em happy.
Scratch those ever-itching ears!
Amplify the Broadway Message . . .
Yes, let's make it crystal clear!

Let's pretend the gospel's friendly
To the flesh and what it craves.
Yes, let's make believe it's pleasant . . .
And then make believe it "saves."

Keep it laid back, mellow, lukewarm;
Preach it Buddy-Buddy, man . . .
Smiley-Faced and Self-affirming,
Life-enhancing on demand.

Share it "soft " . . . more like a pillow
So that feelings won't be hurt.
Keep it lite and inoffensive . . .
Pleasing, cordial, and inert.

Stay away from words like "Holy" . . .
Just caress to show you care.
Keep that "Grace-Thing" easy-breezy
In this kingdom of the air.

Tiptoe past the serpent's garden;
Never ever mention "sin."
Emphasize "the Therapeutic" . . .
And then watch the crowds pour in!

Keep it upbeat, bright, and cheery,
Keep it jolly . . . make it nice!
Push the pastel-sugar feelings . . .
Pull the bloody sacrifice.

———————

Father, please have mercy on us . . .
Sinners blind . . . We want to see!
Take us back, Lord, to the old cross . . .
Take us back to Calvary.

———————

"The problem with America today is not America, it's the church. We have become very shallow as Christians. Very shallow. We have become masters at engineering feelings without much thought."[2] —RAVI ZACHARIAS

SIFTING THROUGH THE RUBBLE

Sadly, the modernist, postmodernist (and now post-postmodernist) eras in the West have been characterized by increasingly hesitant preaching. Over time, in an effort to appear unobtrusively "fair" and nonjudgmental at all cost, the church slowly began to lose her distinctiveness. Her spiritual sharp edges were intentionally dulled. For the past few generations, the church has sounded the shofar of gentle retreat and gladly blended herself into the wallpaper of fundamentalist secularism. She dismantled her own prophetic watchtowers and quietly ceded the cultural battlefield to the advancing legions of "enlightened" religious humanism. She found her comfortable "safe place" under a bushel basket in her designated corner of the room.

As Christian apologist and author Greg Koukl has noted,

> Choosing cultural monasticism rather than hard-thinking advocacy, Christians abandoned the public square to the secularists. When the disciples of Jesus Christ retreated, the disciples of Dewey, Marx, Darwin, Freud, Nietzsche, Skinner, and a host of others replaced them.[1]

Decades ago in 1957, Billy Graham made this observation in one of his evangelistic sermons: "We are living in days of tangled thinking. Purposes, ideals, motives and ideas are all crashing. Lawlessness and revolutions have now become the spirit of the age. And it has penetrated into every realm of human thinking."[2]

(And *those* were "the good old days.")

Some among us saw it coming . . .
When the Gospel left the Square.
Mr. Dewey[3] came out swinging.
Sigmund Freud was everywhere.

When the Bride of Christ retreated,
Nihilism stormed the stage.
Now we're sifting through the rubble
Of the spirit of the age.

Tangled thinking took top billing
With a neo-Marxist spin.
B. F. Skinner got promoted
After Darwin settled in.

"Purpose" proved to be a problem.
Endless compromise was born.
Lawlessness gained legal status.
Truth and meaning? . . . Simply scorned.

Now the culture's steeped in darkness . . .
Quite the bushel basket case.[4]
Now we sing "I Did It My Way."
We've replaced "Amazing Grace."

ENTERTAINMENT SOLD AS WORSHIP

"In my opinion, the great single need of the moment is that light-hearted superficial religionists be struck down with a vision of God high and lifted up, with His train filling the temple. The holy art of worship seems to have passed away like the Shekinah glory from the tabernacle. As a result, we are left to our own devices and forced to make up the lack of spontaneous worship by bringing in countless cheap and tawdry activities to hold the attention of the church people."[1] —A. W. Tozer

"I hope you have become nauseated with the tawdry entertainment that passes for the true worship of God in many of our churches and, like the saints of the past, are longing for more of the deep truths of the inerrant Word of God."[2] —James Montgomery Boice

> Entertainment for the jaded,
> Spotlight singers . . . Center stage!
> We'll be keeping it light-hearted.
> It's the best way to engage.
>
> Yes, we *will* hold your attention,
> Worship studies have been done.
> Some may judge it cheap and tawdry,
> But we call it just plain fun.

Superficial's how we do it!
Sway a bit and keep the beat.
Conjure up that happy feeling;
Come on in and have a seat.

Hollywood invades the temple.
One more latest-greatest thing!
It's a well-thought-out production
Watch it! . . . (There's no need to sing.)

WATCH "THE FALL" NOW FALL FROM FAVOR

> There can be no agreement as to what salvation *is* unless there is agreement as to that from which salvation rescues us. The problem and the solution hang together: the one explicates the other. It is impossible to gain a deep grasp of what the cross achieves without plunging into a deep grasp of what sin is; conversely, to augment one's understanding of the cross is to augment one's understanding of sin. To put the matter another way, sin establishes the plotline of the Bible.[1] —D. A. CARSON

The problem with the world is sin. The problem with the world is first and foremost a spiritual one. The problem is as universal and as personal as it is endemic. The recorded history of mankind is a testament to this sad and poignant truth. The blood, the sweat, and the tears of countless generations give ample evidence to that grim fact. Yet, true to form, we continue to proceed blindly down the path of denial. We are as determined as ever to believe that the problem (i.e., our fallen Adamic nature) must be scrubbed and removed as a concept from our enlightened and progressive public discourse. We have proclaimed our freedom from such an obsolete thought, and we do so proudly. This mindset has been institutionalized. Hollywood, academia, and the bureaucratic halls of government all march in virtual lockstep unison to the secular, amoral drumbeat that resounds throughout Western culture today.

Ironically, and tragically, this trickle-down denial of the fall had its genesis in the seminaries, the pulpits, and the pews. It is there that the salt first turned to sugar and the light grew dim. We have tried to live and govern our lives as though there is no "established plotline."

Watch the Salt turn into sugar
And the fog blot out the Light . . .
Watch the Gospel now surrendered
To the world without a fight.

Watch the intellect go dormant,
Watch the Lord's Beloved snooze.
Watch the Good News be perverted
And the Grace of God confused.

Watch as "feelings" make decisions,
Pragmatism take control . . .
Watch the Holy Spirit's counsel
Be defeated at the polls.

Watch the culture's dissolution,
Fading out before our eyes . . .
Watch the Cheshire Cat there grinning;
Watch as faith now slowly dies.

Watch as Virtue's simply scoffed at,
True Morality ignored . . .
Watch the White Flag Church retreating;
Watch the Truth then be deplored.

Watch The Bride take to the back seat
While Big Brother takes the wheel.
Watch the Gates of Hell swing open
In the Land of Touchy-Feel.

Watch the Word be deconstructed,
Watch tradition being damned . . .
Watch the Nihilistics chuckle
And the silence of the lambs.

Watch "the Fall" now fall from favor
In postmodern clouds of gray,
Watch the jeering Proud parading.
Sin, like magic, falls away.

Watch the church now acquiescing
While it's going with "the flow" . . .
Then watch God 'n' Man evolving . . .
While we tell God where to go.

———————

Lord, You told us to be wary
Of the devil prowling 'round[2] . . .
Give us wisdom and discernment
In this darkness so profound!

May we come to true repentance . . .
Father, help us see your face.[3]
We want Truth . . . not happy feelings
Nor some cheap and easy Grace.

May your Light drive out the darkness.
May we then, Lord, count the cost[4] . . .
Show us Jesus! . . . Father, place us
On our knees before the Cross.

———————

I am astonished that you are so quickly deserting him who called you in the grace of Christ and are turning to a different gospel— not that there is another one, but there are some who trouble you and want to distort the gospel of Christ. But even if we or an angel from heaven should preach to you a gospel contrary to the one we preached to you, let him be accursed. As we have said before, so now I say again: If anyone is preaching to you a gospel contrary to the one you received, let him be accursed. (GALATIANS 1:6–9 ESV)

IN THE LUKEWARM WATER DOLDRUMS

> ... unless the real nature of sin is understood, the gospel cannot be received. The greatness of God's grace will never be grasped unless it is preceded by an understanding of the greatness of sin. . . . What in the Bible makes sin to be sin has disappeared for the great majority of Americans, and the consequence is a massive trivialization of our moral life.[1] —DAVID WELLS

Wells makes an important point. The trivialization of our moral life is not the only thing that is at stake, however. When the church loses sight of "the greatness of [our] sin," the import of the cross and Christ crucified will be trivialized as well.

If we are unable (and/or unwilling) to recognize the depth and magnitude of sin within us (as the Bible clearly teaches), we will eventually see a church unmoored and set adrift, anchorless in the doldrums of spiritual triviality, inconsistency, and incoherence.

If we have adopted and are preaching an "I have a friend in Jesus" message at the expense of an emphasis on God's holiness and His righteous hatred of sin, we deserve the ultimate shipwreck of pop-religion and self-help spirituality that is masquerading as the gospel today in much of Christendom. If we insist upon reading Romans 3:21–22 without the clarifying, foundational backdrop of Romans 3:10–20, we deserve the lukewarm apostate waters that threaten to engulf us.

> "Fallen man is not simply an imperfect creature who needs improvement: he is a rebel who must lay down his arms."[2] —C. S. LEWIS

Sin's the searing of the conscience,
When what's wrong becomes what's right.
It's when Holiness and Virtue's
Brushed aside and out of sight.

Sin's what tells us: "You're the Boss here!"
"There's no 'god' you should obey!"
Simply Pride in us agreeing:
"Yes, God really *didn't* say!"

It's the intellect that reasons
"We're evolving! . . . Give us time!"
It's the attitude proclaiming
"I'm not guilty! . . . There's no crime!"

It's the broad way Jesus warned of,
Dark dressed up to look like light,
It's rebellion at its finest . . .
Man's condition and his plight.

It's the same old Pilate Program,
Truth rejected, left untold.
It's the Idol Calf we covet . . .
For the fool, it's solid gold.

It proclaims: "The Cross is foolish!"
It declares: "It's not my fault!"
One more pampered Sunday morning . . .
It's God's Word without the salt.

It's the lukewarm water doldrums,
It's the Anchor we've replaced
And that empty, sinking feeling
When we shrug at Evil's face.

———————

"The depravity of man is at once the most empirically verifiable reality but at the same time the most intellectually resisted fact."[3] —MALCOLM MUGGERIDGE

LOVE DECLARES JUST CONDEMNATION

The coddled Western church of bright lights and high performance has hit a snag. Social and cultural "relevance" has elbowed holiness, righteousness, and repentance off the auditorium stage. The gospel of grace and the necessary bad news that must necessarily precede it have become increasingly and noticeably absent in our comfort-driven, "Me First," "Me, Too," and "Have It Your Way" world.

Decades ago, C. S. Lewis recognized that "Christianity now has to preach the diagnosis—in itself very bad news—before it can win the hearing for the cure."[1]

Theologian and author Michael Horton puts it this way:

> We must be stripped of our fig leaves in order to be clothed with Christ's righteousness so we can stand in the judgment of a holy God. The question is whether the aim of ministry today is to tear off our fig leaves so we can be clothed with Christ or to help us add a few more.[2]

The tough love preaching of true biblical Christianity, the kind of preaching that penetrates beyond skin-deep and slices boldly into the hearts of blind and wicked sinners, has become exceedingly rare. The sharp, double-edged sword of the gospel truth has become a blunted palette knife of pleasing, "Do Not Disturb" pastel colors.

The apostle Paul wrote and placed the first three and a half chapters of the epistle to the Romans at the beginning of his treatise, after all. He did so for a purpose. The gospel of redemption requires that all our precious fig leaves be removed before the message of the cross can be truly heard.

———

Love declares "There's no one righteous!"
Love declares "Bridge out ahead!"
Love declares that there's a Savior,
While the world's way wants you dead.

Love declares the very bad news . . .
True Love makes it crystal clear.
Love declares just condemnation
And a Holy God to fear.

———————

Sin will tell you "Love's not like that!"
Pride proclaims "I'm Number One!"
Sin says "Strive for Self-fulfillment!"
Sin insists . . . "My will be done!"

Sin says "Here's another fig leaf!"
Wear it very proudly, friend.
Fig leaves keep us from exposure
Right up to the very end.

———————

Love, though, shares true revelation—
Yes, no matter what the cost.
Son, the world will hate you for it.
You want proof? . . . Observe the Cross.

———————

As a result, we are no longer to be children, tossed here and there by waves and carried about by every wind of doctrine, by the trickery of men, by craftiness in deceitful scheming; but speaking the truth in love, we are to grow up in all *aspects* into Him who is the head, *even* Christ. (EPHESIANS 4:14–15 NASB)

Living Water Living

"Anyone who is thirsty may come to me!

Anyone who believes in me may come and drink!

For the Scriptures declare,

'Rivers of living water will flow from his heart.'"

(JOHN 7:37–38 NLT)

EVERYBODY'S CHASING HAPPY

"I didn't go to religion to make me happy. I always knew a bottle of Port would do that. If you want a religion to make you feel really comfortable, I certainly don't recommend Christianity."[1] —C. S. LEWIS

"Aim at heaven and you will get earth thrown in. Aim at earth and you get neither."[2] —C. S. LEWIS

———

Everybody's chasing Happy.
Happy seems to be "The Thing."
Yes, Proud Pleasure is the treasure
That keeps challenging The King.

It's a temporal endeavor . . .
Just like clockwork . . . going strong.
Adam chased it in the Garden
And we've followed right along.

It's what everybody's after
Here beneath the noonday sun.
It's a vapor . . . just a shadow
After all is said and done.

Happy's now our main objective.
Self-fulfillment is our aim.
"It's about me" is our motto;
It's the Golden Calf we claim.

———

Will "the Pleasure" hounds keep sniffing
After Satan's Calves of Gold?[1]
Will the search keep on proceeding?
Will we buy the Lie he sold?

Will this great big world impede us?
Will these vanities prevail?
Has the lust for things and pleasure
Now become our Holy Grail?

Will these vanities that rule us
Have the final say, my friend?
Will these fleeting satisfactions
Satisfy us in the end?

As Forever fast approaches,
Will we have the time to turn?
Will the pleasures we now treasure
Be our Number One concern?

———————

I denied myself nothing my eyes desired;
    I refused my heart no pleasure.
My heart took delight in all my labor,
    and this was the reward for all my toil.
Yet when I surveyed all that my hands had done
    and what I had toiled to achieve,
everything was meaningless, a chasing after the wind;
    nothing was gained under the sun.

(ECCLESIASTES 2:10–11)

LORD, REVEAL OUR DESTITUTION

David was furious. "As surely as the LORD lives," he vowed, "any man who would do such a thing deserves to die! He must repay four lambs to the poor man for the one he stole and for having no pity."

Then Nathan said to David, "You are that man!" (2 SAMUEL 12:5–7 NLT)

"These 'depths' in which we sometimes find ourselves . . . come upon us not by misfortune but by God's providential hand in order that we might learn to know ourselves as we are before him and to seek his grace and forgiveness."[1] —DAVID WELLS

Lord, please help us see the damage
Lying scattered in our wake.
Grant us, Lord, Divine affliction[2] . . .
Help us own this Grim Mistake.

Send us Nathans to confront us;[3]
Help us see the Sin denied . . .
Shine the light of Truth, Lord, on us;
Come and find us . . . where we hide.[4]

Grant the Grace of true contrition,[5]
Help us see with honest eyes.
Help us know You, wholly Holy,
Help us shed these alibis.

May the words of Jesus haunt us ...
May they truly track us down.
May they first bring grief and sorrow,[6]
Show us lost before we're found.[7]

May they make us truly mournful,[8]
Make us meek[9] with deep regret,
Poor in spirit, hungry, thirsting[10] ...
Yes, imprisoned,[11] lost in debt.

Help us know sin's condemnation[12]
So we'll know Amazing Grace ...
Help us turn from this, our darkness,
Then to see sweet Mercy's Face.

Help us know we're dead in Adam,[13]
Yes, before there's life in Christ ...
Help us fathom this Provision:
His atoning sacrifice.[14]

Lord, reveal our destitution,
In the mourning help us know.
At the dawn,[15] please, Shepherd, find us,
In this broken world below.

Holy Spirit, give us vision,
Give us Light to know The Way[16] ...
Take us to the Cross of Calv'ry,
Where the nighttime turns to day.

Father, call us to repentance,
Slay us there on bended knee.
Show us why the Lamb and Shepherd
Fought to climb Golgotha's Tree.[17]

Help us see there first and foremost,
Our uncleanness[18] in your sight . . .
Filthy rags[19] turned into riches,
Sealed[20] in Resurrected Christ!

———

Now I am glad I sent it, not because it hurt you, but because the pain caused you to repent and change your ways. It was the kind of sorrow God wants his people to have, so you were not harmed by us in any way. For the kind of sorrow God wants us to experience leads us away from sin and results in salvation. There's no regret for that kind of sorrow. But worldly sorrow, which lacks repentance, results in spiritual death. (2 CORINTHIANS 7:9–10 NLT)

HAS THE TRUTH BEEN SUPERSEDED?

Has what's true been superseded
By the way you feel today?
Is the Inner Child still reigning
In this broken jar of clay?

Has the Self been elevated?
Are you climbing higher still?
Can you claw your way to heaven
Overlooking Calv'ry's hill?

Were you born into His Kingdom?
Grafted in by grace alone?
Are you striving in your own strength
To place *your* Self on the throne?

DID YOU TIP THAT RIGHTEOUS SCALE?

"Our conduct is not the basis for our salvation, but is influenced by our salvation."[1] —JOHN M. FRAME

————

Did your good works make you Holy,
"God-acceptable," my friend?
Did you work hard for salvation?
Will it save you in the end?

Did you meet the Law's requirements?
Did your conduct make the grade?
Were you close enough to kosher
To erase the mess you made?

Were your thoughts quite "good enough," sir?
Did you tip that "Righteous Scale"?
Did you meet your expectations?
Did you pass . . . or did you fail?

Were you graded on the curve, sir?
Did you give yourself a break?
Did you overlook a few things . . .
Like the Cross . . . for Heaven's sake?

————

All our righteousnesses *are* like filthy rags;
We all fade as a leaf,
And our iniquities, like the wind,
Have taken us away. (ISAIAH 64:6 NJKV)

"There is none righteous, no, not one." (ROMANS 3:10 NKJV)

MAYBE IF WE'RE HONEST

"If only there were evil people somewhere insidiously committing evil deeds, and it were necessary only to separate them from the rest of us and destroy them."[1]
—ALEXANDR SOLZHENITSYN

————

Look at them, the "evil people,"
Making life so awful here.
They're the ones who need removing.
They're the ones we need to fear.

Yes, they're causing all the trouble,
Filled with hate, beyond repair.
They're deplorable and wicked . . .
Isolate them over there.

There they are . . . the trouble-makers!
Brutish beasts from head to toe.
They're the guilty ones, we're certain.
They're the ones who have to go!

————

Maybe . . . (if we turn around, sir)
We might recognize we're lost.
Maybe truth will then confront us.
At the foot of Calv'ry's Cross.

Who knows? . . . Maybe . . . (if we're honest)
There's a lesson here to learn.
Maybe there's message for us,
A Redeemer to discern.

——————

Jews demand signs and Greeks look for wisdom, but we preach Christ crucified: a stumbling block to Jews and foolishness to Gentiles, but to those whom God has called, both Jews and Greeks, Christ the power of God and the wisdom of God. (1 CORINTHIANS 1:22–24)

——————

"Shallow honesty seeks 'sharing,' deep honesty seeks Truth. Shallow honesty stands in the presence of others—deep honesty stands in the presence of God."[2]
—PETER KREEFT

SIMPLE PARABLES OF BEAUTY

Jesus, God incarnate, used parables to disclose liberating spiritual truth to those with ears to hear. The Word used words to touch the heart and soul and quicken the spirit of fallen man. But we are also drawn to the truth by seeing. We are surrounded every day, here and now, by *visual* parables that speak to us in different ways, sublime parables of beauty, majesty, and splendor that help to illumine the pathway home to the creative Author of the universe and his eternal kingdom.

Pastor and author Steve DeWitt has written:

> Created beauty eclipses God's beauty in the desire factory of man's heart. It is a case of mistaken identity. Every created beauty was created by God to lead our affections to Him. That's why He made the pleasures of earthly beauty so fleeting—so that on the other side of the pleasure we might experience either wonder and worship and ultimate satisfaction in God or the pursuit of the pleasure that beauty provides for its own sake. If we choose the latter, we will only be disappointed again.[1]

And C. S. Lewis amplifies

> We do not want merely to see beauty ... we want something else which can hardly be put into words—to be united with the beauty we see, to pass into it, to receive it into ourselves, to bathe in it, to become part of it. That is why we have peopled air and earth and water with gods and goddesses, and nymphs and elves."[2]

————

Simple parables of Beauty
To be seen instead of heard . . .
One more way The Way is speaking,
One more way the spirit's stirred.

Simple parables of Beauty
That surround us every day
Speak the words of natural Wonder
And invite us home to stay.

Simple parables of vision,
Double-edged swords of Light . . .
From the Author and Creator
Of the True, the Good, the Right.

Perfect peace, eternal comfort,
Truth sublime by sight revealed . . .
Living Water set before us,
Drawing souls to what is Real.

Hear creation's silent whisper,
Truth that no one can deny.
Revelation . . . Beauty beckons
Us to wonder and delight.

Hear the Shepherd by still water,
Silent whispers on the breeze.
Hear the Bridegroom's first proposal
In reflection on your knees.

SOMEONE, QUICK! GO FIND JOSIAH!

> When they were bringing out the money which had
> been brought into the house of the LORD, Hilkiah the
> priest found the book of the law of the LORD *given* by
> Moses. . . .
>
> When the king heard the words of the law, he tore
> his clothes. (2 CHRONICLES 34:14, 19 NASB)

———

Scripture records the repeated failure of the Hebrew nation to honor the word of God given to them through Moses. Time after time the people turned their back on the Law of Moses, and as a consequence the nation fell into prolonged periods of apostasy and wickedness. Time after time they neglected the commands of the true and living God who had brought them out of Egypt. Instead, they chased after other gods, the pagan deities of the nations that surrounded them. They worshipped idols, and their hearts grew hard and cold. And the result was always the same: calamity, moral chaos, defeat, and destruction.

In the second book of Chronicles, we are told that Hilkiah, the high priest, discovered the long-neglected book of the law in the disrepair and rubble of the temple in Jerusalem. He brushed the dust off, removed the cobwebs, and brought the long-forgotten sacred scroll to King Josiah. We are told that Josiah, recognizing the guilt of the nation, "tore his clothes" in mourning and immediately called the people to true repentance.

Nothing much has changed today.

We live in a prideful age. We have set God's Word aside, neglected for the most part and gathering dust.

Satan's scheme, his clever trap, is to twist reality and bend the truth for his own wicked aim and good pleasure. He is more than happy to convince all of us that we are hapless victims. He awards us with blue ribbon, "True Victim" status, and hands out perpetual "Get out of jail free" grievance cards. And then he fans the flames of our own self-righteousness: the icing on his cake.

He camouflages our guilt and then deceitfully pretends to set us "free." Afterward, he slithers off into the underbrush to watch the bloodletting.

Where is Hilkiah when we need him?

Where is Josiah?

———————

> Everybody's now a victim;
> Satan swears we're off the hook!
> Pointing fingers at each other . . .
> (No one's pointing at The Book).

———————

> Someone, quick! . . . Go find Josiah!
> Tell him what Hilkiah found
> In this deconstructed rubble.
> Tell him there's still solid ground.
>
> Tell him that the Law's not finished,
> Tell him that it's judging still.
> Yes, God's Law remains the tutor[1]
> Pointing us to Calv'ry's hill.

———————

"Therefore the Law has become our tutor *to lead us* to Christ, so that we may be justified by faith." (GALATIANS 3:24 NASB)

———

"Before God can give us the gospel, He must slay us in the law. But as he does so, he shows us that the law contains the gospel and points us to it,"[2] —JAMES MONTGOMERY BOICE

HE'S PHILOSOPHY'S CONUNDRUM

Who is this Jesus?

The philosophers, the religious, the learned scholars throughout history have tried to tag, corral, and define him on (and in) their own terms. But Jesus always evades mere worldly definitions and understanding. He escapes the time-bound grasp of the haughty, powerful, and wise. He shocks and challenges the intellect beyond mere stretching. He breaks all the rules of human reason—and yet somehow remains the most reasonable One of all.

He is known through revelation—never by charts and graphs or cleverly devised deductions and formulas. He befuddled and confounded two thousand years ago, and He still does so today.

———

He's philosophy's conundrum,
He's religion's pesky thorn . . . ,
He's a stumbling block, a myst'ry,
And the Way to be reborn.

He's the Answer to the question
Nicodemus nearly missed . . .
He's where all the prophets pointed.
He's where "Love" and "Holy" kiss.

He's why Pharisees still tremble,
He's why Sadducees complain,
He's the One who frustrates scholars,
And the One the world disdains.

He's why mourners dance at daybreak,
Why the poor in spirit sing,
He's the Morning Star of Promise—
Good News that His servants bring.

He's the One who stirs the spirit
Of the sinner who repents . . .
The Eternal Life that's waiting,
Grace and Mercy Heaven sent.

———————

. . . assuming that you have heard of the stewardship of God's grace that was given to me for you, how the mystery was made known to me by revelation, as I have written briefly. When you read this, you can perceive my insight into the mystery of Christ, which was not made known to the sons of men in other generations as it has now been revealed to his holy apostles and prophets by the Spirit. (EPHESIANS 3:2–5 ESV)

YES, THE PROPHETS SAW HIM COMING

Fools will dismiss it, skeptics will doubt it, and mockers will scoff at it, but the true, living, and eternal God of all creation opened a window of light into this dark, fallen, and time-bound world and spoke a laser-like beam of Hope into it. In the Old Testament, God truly projected a glorious, cross-shaped, prophetic "shadow" into and through Jewish history, a shadow that spread across the landscape of the Levant. It was there that God introduced His Righteous plan of redemption for all of humanity . . . a gift of Amazing Grace given birth into the world through the nation of Israel, . . . the gift of God incarnate, Prophet, Priest, and King. God provided a Savior.

All the prophets saw Him coming . . . and they saw Him coming yet again.

————

Concerning this salvation, the prophets who prophesied about the grace that was to be yours searched and inquired carefully, inquiring what person or time the Spirit of Christ in them was indicating when he predicted the sufferings of Christ and the subsequent glories. (1 PETER 1:10–11 ESV)

————

God of Glory cast a Shadow:
Pentateuch to Malachi . . .
Moses wrote of Him in Eden[1]
And when Isaac didn't die.[2]

Prophets spoke of Him foreshadowed
As that first Passover Lamb.[3]
Blood applied for man's redemption . . .
Burning bush, the Word, I AM.

He was pictured in the desert
In the midst of wand'ring souls . . .
There! . . . God's sacrificial system
In a cloud the Truth unfolds.

There the story was presented
In that tabernacle tent.
There His Grace and there His Glory . . .
Truth Incarnate to be sent.

Law and Grace there found expression
Revelation! . . . Reason's rhyme.
Scripture spoke of his arrival . . .
The Eternal One in time.

Theirs the gift true God has given . . .
Theirs the Blessing we've received.
Theirs the Holy Door discovered . . .
Abram heard it . . . and believed.[4]

Did you notice Him in Joseph?
There the Savior was displayed.[5]
There the Bread of Life provided.
Brethren then by Grace amazed.[6]

David witnessed Him triumphant,[7]
Malachi was shown the end.[8]
Ruth as well has told His story,
Yes, when Boaz took her in.[9]

Prophet Daniel knew the timing.[10]
Prophet Micah knew just where.[11]...
Yes, Isaiah saw the suff'ring[12]
Of God's Lamb our sins to bear.[13]

May God's Spirit find us willing...
May the hungry heart still seek.[14]
Give us Abrahamic faith, Lord
To believe the Word You speak.[15]

Help us follow, Lord, this shadow[16]
To the Glory of the Son...
May our pride and skepticism
Once for all be overcome.

Make us meek, indeed, like Moses[17];
Make us tremble... Make us quake.[18]
May we mourn like Jeremiah...
For our sins... for Heaven's sake.

———

"For no prophecy was ever produced by the will of
man, but men spoke from God as they were carried
along by the Holy Spirit." (2 PETER 1:21 ESV)

IN OBSCURITY THEY FOUND HIM

"But when the fullness of time had come, God sent forth his Son, born of woman, born under the law."
(GALATIANS 4:4 ESV)

For centuries the prophets of Israel had written about a future Savior, a deliverer, a coming King. From Genesis to Malachi this "anointed One" was promised. Major and minor prophets alike for at least 1500 years had pointed expectantly to this Messiah. And the Hebrew people waited and waited until, in God's perfect timing, He appeared just as was predicted, just where He was predicted, and just when He was predicted. As one Bible scholar and author has put it,

> This Promised One of the Old Testament scriptures appeared in the little village of Bethlehem in the Judean hills of the obscure land of Israel. It was the noon hour of human history—it was the fullness of time (Galatians 4:4). The infinite, eternal Creator was now walking among His creation.[1]

And the rest is history.

All the prophets saw Him coming
Down the corridor of time.
They foretold the King's appearing
And their words were all aligned.

In the foothills of Judea,
In the town of Bethlehem,
Shepherds first beheld His glory,
And they bowed to worship Him.

In obscurity they found Him.
They beheld the Lamb of God!
Humble shepherds gathered 'round Him
Dazed, amazed . . . profoundly awed.

It was written in the Scriptures;
Yes, for centuries they knew.
Now at last, here in a manger
All the prophecies came true.

Now the bondage might be broken,
Those condemned could be set free.
Death and darkness lay defeated . . .
Swallowed up in victory![2]

Born, incarnate King of Glory,
Zion's Hope . . . the Promised One! . . .
There! Emanuel . . . Messiah!
God's true Light, the Father's Son.

HOLD ME UP TO HIS EXAMPLE

We've all seen it and heard it before: the persistent accusatory and judgmental finger pointing aimed at the "hypocrisy of Christians." It is the great skeptical dodge of those who dismiss the truth of the Christian gospel, because: "Well," they say, "just look at those Christians! They're nothing like the Jesus I've read about! How DARE they persist in their proselytizing and annoying pronouncements! We can see right through their spiritual charade, their moral failures, and their bogus 'good news' pomposity! I could never be a part of it! They're all a bunch of hypocrites!"

For the most part, this predictable protestation is the time-tested, classic smokescreen of Self-preservation, spiritual evasion of the first order, and an indication that the Bible's central message is right on target: we are ALL in desperate need of a Savior.

Please DO judge me next to Jesus—
Point that finger as you please.
I don't measure up . . . I know that.
I've been driven to my knees.

Please DO hold me to that Standard,
Make me poor in spirit,[1] friend.
Make me hunger to be righteous . . .
Make me thirst . . . then thirst again.[2]

Hold me up to Christ's example,
Read me Romans chapter three.[3]
Help this blind man get the picture . . .
By true Grace and Honesty.

Bring in Nathan if you have to.[4]
Please produce in me despair.
Make me mourn these filthy rags,[5] sir.
Please, my "feelings" do not spare.

Please expose each sin within me . . .
Yes, remind me ev'ry day!
Shine His Light of Truth right through me . . .
Drive me home . . . the Narrow Way.[6]

———

"Blessed are the poor in spirit,
    for theirs is the kingdom of heaven.
Blessed are those who mourn,
    for they will be comforted.
Blessed are the meek,
    for they will inherit the earth.
Blessed are those who hunger and thirst
      for righteousness,
    for they will be filled." (MATTHEW 5:3–6)

———

It's no disgrace to Christianity, it is no disgrace to any great religion, that its counsels of perfection have not made every single person perfect. If after centuries a disparity is still found between its ideal and its followers, it only means that the religion still maintains the ideal, and the followers still need it.[7] —G. K. CHESTERTON

TRUTH MAY SIMPLY SAY "I AM"

Christ is the Way, the Truth, and the Life. His claims
on our belief are absolute. If we flinch at this point; If
our trumpet gives an uncertain sound; if we present a
Christ who is inoffensive, because He is after all only
one perspective among many; if we allow the enemies
of truth to dictate the terms of engagement; if, in other
words, we compromise on the issue of truth, then we
betray the next generation to unrelieved darkness. If
we do this then may God have mercy on their souls—
and more so on ours.[1] —DONALD WILLIAMS

———

Jesus claims to be the Truth, sir . . .
Cornerstone and Bottom Line.
Mercy's Light of Revelation
For the guilty and the blind.

Truth may sometimes point like Nathan
Or stand silent like a lamb . . .
Truth may simply stare right through you.
Truth may simply say "I AM."

Truth devolved from "Yes!" to "Maybe"
In the wink of Satan's eye.
Then from "Maybe" to "I doubt it"
And from there to "Crucify!"

That's the dark the sinner hides in,
That's the tar pit that we found.
That's the curse that we're now stuck with,
That's the Fall we all fell down.

———

But the Truth lives on forever,
That's the truth—we have no doubt.
He's the Life, the Resurrection . . .
Truth we cannot live without.

———

"Jesus said to him, 'I am the way, and the truth, and the life. No one comes to the Father except through me.'" (JOHN 14:6 ESV)

HE'S THE JUSTICE MAN IS DREADING

Those who do not meet [God] clothed in his gift of salvation and grace must meet Him naked without a wedding garment. For all must meet Him, for He is Truth, and the Truth is universal and unavoidable. Mercy is Truth clothed; judgment is Truth naked.[1] —PETER KREEFT

He's the naked Truth most Holy,
Calling honest men to turn . . .
Witness fools in dark denial . . .
Watch his invitation spurned.

He's the Judge of sin and sinners . . .
Of the proud who will not bend,
Showing mercy to the mournful,[2]
Poor in spirit He defends.[3]

He's the reason we know Evil
When it rears its ugly head . . .
He's the Righteous Judge Omniscient
Of the living and the dead.[4]

He's the One who gave fair warning
When He set the bar so high.
He's the Narrow Gate to glory
And why "good works" just won't fly.

He's the One who sees right through us,
He's the One who knows the heart . . .
He's the One by whom we're measured,
Who has Mercy to impart.[5]

He's the Justice man is dreading,
Brought to light in ancient creeds,
He's the nemesis of sinners,
Holy-Love the sinner needs.

————

The assurance of Heaven is never given to the person. And that's why at the core of the Christian faith is the grace of God. If there's one word I would grab from all of that, it's forgiveness—that you can be forgiven. I can be forgiven, and it is of the grace of God. But once you understand that, I think the ramifications are world-wide.[6] —RAVI ZACHARIAS

BANKING ON A CAKE WALK?

Were you told the Way was easy?
Did you think "Prosperity!"?
Were you promised blue skies only?
(No one mentioned Calvary?)

When He called you, sir, to follow,
Did you overlook His pain?
Did you miss the way He suffered,
Disregard that crimson stain?

Did you think the world would love you
If you truly called him "Lord"?
Did they promise only comfort
If you dared to wield the Sword?

Were you banking on a Cake Walk?
Did you really count the cost?
Is there Truth out there to follow?
Are you clinging to the Cross?

"Then Jesus said to his disciples, 'If any of you wants to be my follower, you must give up your own way, take up your cross, and follow me.'" (MATTHEW 16:24 NLT)

FURNACE OF AFFLICTION

In the book of Job, Zophar gives Job well-intentioned but faulty spiritual counsel. With a proud air of self-assurance, he tells Job that his suffering and affliction have come upon him because of some personal sin he had committed, and that he must repent to find relief. In reality, however, the sufferings of Job were sovereignly ordained by God for even higher and more mysterious purposes . . . to purify Job's faith and to manifest God's power and glory for the benefit of others.

> "It may be the divine purpose—that we ourselves shall be *benefited* by our trouble. No human life ever reaches its best possibilities without pain and cost. . . . Sometimes we are called to suffer for the sake of others—that they may be made better." Beware the yeast[1] —J. R. MILLER (1905)

> ———

> "Fire never hurts the gold . . . it only purifies it and removes the dross."[2] —EUGENE NATION

> If your counsel comes from Zophar,[3]
> Take it with a grain of salt.
> Yes, be very, very wary . . .
> This pain may not be your fault.
>
> In God's sov'reign plan it could be
> Simply what has been ordained.
> In the furnace of affliction,
> Friend, the purest gold's obtained.

Tribulation's white-hot pressure
May indeed remove the dross . . .
Pre-determined quite divinely
Bearing witness to the Cross.

Lord, come hell or come high water,
May we trust in You alone.
Purify our faith in suff'ring,
Lead us to the Cornerstone . . .

One day we'll be golden vessels
In the Presence of the King,
And with angels we'll surround Him.
Clouds of witnesses will sing.

LORD, PUT DOWN THIS GRIM REBELLION

Now when Jesus came into the district of Caesarea Philippi, he asked his disciples, "Who do people say that the Son of Man is?" And they said, "Some say John the Baptist, others say Elijah, and others Jeremiah or one of the prophets." He said to them, "But who do you say that I am?" Simon Peter replied, "You are the Christ, the Son of the living God." And Jesus answered him, "Blessed are you, Simon Bar-Jonah! For flesh and blood has not revealed this to you, but my Father who is in heaven. And I tell you, you are Peter, and on this rock I will build my church, and the gates of hell shall not prevail against it. I will give you the keys of the kingdom of heaven, and whatever you bind on earth shall be bound in heaven, and whatever you loose on earth shall be loosed in heaven." Then he strictly charged the disciples to tell no one that he was the Christ. (MATTHEW 16:13–20 ESV)

———

Immediately after Jesus warned his disciples to "be on your guard against the yeast [i.e., the false teaching] of the Pharisees and Sadducees,"[1] He took them to a third spot where spiritual deception lurked—a place called Caesarea Philippi (aka "The Gates of Hades," the entrance to the spirits of the underground).

Here was a place that had for centuries attracted Greco-Roman pagan revelry, "religious" revelry raised to a fevered pitch. It was a place where the senses were stoked and glorified and where unbridled sexual appetites were indulged and gratified. It was where the goat-footed, horned god of the underworld (Pan) was honored and worshiped, where temple prostitution was part of the religious "service," where human sacrifice was a sacred rite, and where "porneia" was extolled as an exalted path to enlightenment. It was an idolatrous playground for the lustful, the "liberated," and the licentious sophisticates of the age . . . the "with it" and the "woke."

Caesarea Philippi was the jet-set "place to be" and the best the sensate world had to offer for those "in the know." Here was the first century's version of Hollywood, Las Vegas, steamy brothels, and late-term abortion clinics all rolled into one neat "spiritual" package. Unapologetic, sneering and leering, debauched, spiritual perversion on proud display . . .

It was here, surrounded by this Dionysian darkness, that Jesus turned to his disciples and asked: "But what about you? . . . Who do you say I am?"

To which Peter, son of Jonah, answered, "You are the Christ, the Son of the living God."

---

1) Beware the yeast of the Pharisees (The Law/works righteousness).
2) Beware the yeast of the Sadducees (The human intellect alone/spiritual compromise).
3) Beware the yeast of the fallen world (pleasures of the flesh—hedonism/narcissism).

Lord, You warned the Way is narrow,[2]
And You said, "I am The Gate."[3]
Take us please, Lord, up to Calv'ry;
Give us Grace to mourn our state.[4]

Give us eyes to see[5] . . . like Peter;
Help us see what Peter saw!
Lord, put down this grim rebellion[6] . . .
Teach us through your Holy Law.[7]

Take away the world's deception,
Help us overcome[8] the lies . . .
Turn us, Lord, from fatal error;
Grant us Grace to see our Pride.[9]

Bless us with true revelation.[10]
Father, help us hear and heed . . .
True Light, penetrate this darkness,
Give us, Lord, the Kingdom's key.[11]

Gift of Faith, Lord, plant within us.[12]
Father, break the devil's spell . . .
Truth, be known! . . . Release the prisoners![13]
Take us from these Gates of Hell.[14]

Give us ears to hear your calling . . .
Help us, Lord, beware the yeast.
May we one day see the Bridegroom
At the Father's Wedding Feast.[15]

THERE'S A ROMANCE FROM THE START

"Listen . . . with all your might; hear the living and active word. The teaching and preaching of God's imperishable word is truly a sacred event whereby the Truth penetrates hearts and minds, consciences are quickened, sin is disclosed, salvation is offered, wisdom is imparted . . . [I]f we listen, if we actively engage ourselves in hearing, if we participate as the Holy Spirit works in our midst . . .[1] —DOUGLAS GROOTHUIS

———

For this reason we also thank God without ceasing, because when you received the word of God which you heard from us, you welcomed *it* not *as* the word of men, but as it is in truth, the word of God, which also effectively works in you who believe. (1 THESSALONIANS 2:13 NKJV)

"So then faith *comes* by hearing, and hearing by the word of God." (ROMANS 10:17 NKJV)

———

There's a Living Word at work here,
Yes, true Language from the Heart . . .
There's a Maker, there's a Reason,
There's a Romance from the Start.

Listen closely . . . there's true Meaning
That transcends the world we're in . . .
There's a Lover who is waiting,
Christ who overcomes our sin.

He's the Perfect Lamb, a Person,
He's the Plan you may have heard,
God Incarnate, Son and Bridegroom . . .
His proposal's in the Word.

———————

"Truly, truly, I say to you, whoever hears my word and believes him who sent me has eternal life. He does not come into judgment, but has passed from death to life." (JOHN 5:24 ESV)

WHERE THE CUTTING EDGE OF JUSTICE . . .

"So He drove out the man; and He placed cherubim at the east of the garden of Eden, and a flaming sword which turned every way, to guard the way to the tree of life." (GENESIS 3:24 NKJV)

"And take the helmet of salvation and the sword of the Spirit, which is the word of God." (EPHESIANS 6:17 NKJV)

———

During the third century before the birth of Christ, the Romans discovered a way to make a sharp, double-edged sword. The sword was called a *gladius*. It was made of tempered steel, was usually two to three feet long, and its razor-sharp edges tapered to a deadly, penetrating point. At the time, the gladius revolutionized the art of warfare, and with it the Roman legion was virtually unstoppable as it swept through the Mediterranean world in conquest.

In the New Testament book of Hebrews, the author (quite possibly the apostle Paul) describes a different kind of "double-edged sword," the Spirit-breathed Word of truth—i.e., the *gladius* of God:

For the word of God *is* living and powerful, and sharper than any two-edged sword, piercing even to the division of soul and spirit, and of joints and marrow, and is a discerner of the thoughts and intents of the heart. (HEBREWS 4:12 NKJV)

The armies of Rome battled for physical territory, influence, and power in the temporal realm (as all the "Caesars" of the world still do today). But, according to Scripture, there is a much more serious battle being waged around us. For the most part, the conflict goes undetected and unacknowledged. It is not a battle of flesh and blood, nor is it a battle waged primarily for political power, ideological influence, or imperial gain. No, the Bible speaks of a *spiritual* battle—a *spiritual war*. The Bible tells us of a conflict that has been raging since before the creation of the world, a conflict that has subsequently spilled over into the realm of human affairs and human history. It teaches that *this* war is not *just* a temporal conflict. It is much more than that. It is personal, universal, eternal, and a matter of life and death.

The Word (the *gladius* of God) informs us that the battle lines are drawn between the spiritual forces of good and those of evil. The lines are drawn between the spiritual forces of darkness and the spiritual forces of light, between life-giving Truth and deadly spiritual deception. God's Word reveals that the battle is not being waged for square miles of territory, strategic oil fields, or other prime strategic real estate. The battlefield in no way resembles the rolling countryside of Gettysburg, the beaches of Normandy, or the plains of Carchemish. Indeed, this unseen battle is for the eternal souls of fallen man, and each and every individual is engaged, whether he or she realizes or likes it.

Today skeptics, liberal scholars, and many "progressive" theologians would have us believe that the Bible is little more than man's dull and stammering attempt to describe an impersonal, obscure, and silent deity. The scholars would like us to believe that the Old and New Testament Scriptures, from Genesis to Revelation, were written by men who were simply doing their best to record their thoughts *about* God and what they imagined God to be like. The actual Scriptures, of course, teach something radically different. The

Bible claims to be God's Word about man, not man's word about God. The Bible claims to be divinely initiated, prophetic, God-breathed verbal communication to sinful man, specifically and intentionally delivered to stir man's heart and mind first to an *awareness* of his unholy, sinful condition, and then to quicken him to seek salvation through repentance and faith in Jesus, the Messiah—a profound gift of mercy and grace.

"The "gladius of God" claims to be divine *revelation*, intelligently designed and empowered to *stab* the conscience of man to life and then to prod him along the way (the narrow Way) to the glorious promise of eternal life. It is a powerful sword with two edges: Holy Truth and Justice on one side and Mercy and Grace on the other—honed and tapered to a very specific, penetrating point. The Sword of Truth is adversarial and dangerous. It can penetrate to the heart of the matter with a single, quick, and deadly thrust. Indeed, it threatens to kill the prideful, self-centered, autonomous rebel who reigns within us.

Father, help us get the picture
By the true Light from above . . .
Where the cutting edge of Justice
Meets the edge of Grace and Love.

With your Sword, dear Lord, come show us
What's inside and what is true.
Come, divide the soul and spirit . . .
With your Word, Lord, run us through!

May each edge of Revelation
Cut through all our alibis.
Sword of Truth, come pierce the darkness;
Bring true Light to blinded eyes.

May the Holy Law convict us,
Judging attitude and thought.
Father, cut us to the marrow
By the Word your Spirit brought.

There the edge of Holy Justice
Meets the edge of Mercy's Love,
Christ, the tapered tip of Glory . . .
Lamb of God sent from above.

Calvary! . . . the Cross of Jesus!
That's the Point! . . . in Christ revealed!
Penetrate each heart of darkness . . .
Then through Faith, Sweet Spirit, seal.

May the Law and Truth cut deeply!
Holy Justice, lay us bare.
Lord, reveal our Sinful nature . . .
Holy Spirit, take us there.

———————

"And to the angel of the church in Pergamum write: 'The words of him who has the sharp two-edged sword . . .

He who has an ear, let him hear what the Spirit says to the churches. To the one who conquers I will give some of the hidden manna, and I will give him a white stone, with a new name written on the stone that no one knows except the one who receives it.'" (REVELATION 2:12, 17 ESV)

WILL WE DWELL WITHIN HIS TENT?

"And behold, the curtain of the temple was torn in two, from top to bottom. And the earth shook, and the rocks were split." (MATTHEW 27:51 ESV)

Do you not know? Do you not hear?
    Has it not been told you from the beginning?
    Have you not understood from the foundations
        of the earth?
It is he who sits above the circle of the earth,
    and its inhabitants are like grasshoppers;
who stretches out the heavens like a curtain,
    and spreads them like a tent to dwell in.

                        (ISAIAH 40:21–22 ESV)

Will we see creation's curtain
Torn asunder once for all?
Will the heavens then be parted
As the stars begin to fall?[1]

Will God's Glory then astound us
Like the lightning east to west.
Is the Morning Star proclaiming
Soon we'll be forever blessed?

Will the true light chase the darkness?
Will the nighttime flee at last?
Will God's mercy then embrace us?
Will these tears be in our past?

Will the Bridegroom find us waiting
Dressed in linen gleaming white?
Will the Son then dawn upon us?
Will our lamps be full that night?

Will the greater Son of David
Come again to gain the throne?
Is our Blessed Hope approaching[2]—
New Creation's Cornerstone?

Did we recognize the shadow
When that veil in two was rent?
Do you know Him? . . . Do you love Him?
Will we dwell within His tent?

I'M A PERFECT ROMANS SEVEN

The premier answer to the question What's wrong with the world? What's wrong with the church? is not politics, the economy, secularism, sectarianism, globalization or global warming . . . none of these, as significant as they are. As Chesterton wrote, the answer to the question 'What's wrong with the world?' is just two words: "I am."[1] —CARDINAL TIMOTHY DOLAN

We know that the law is spiritual; but I am unspiritual, sold as a slave to sin. I do not understand what I do. For what I want to do I do not do, but what I hate I do. And if I do what I do not want to do, I agree that the law is good. As it is, it is no longer I myself who do it, but it is sin living in me. For I know that good itself does not dwell in me, that is, in my sinful nature. For I have the desire to do what is good, but I cannot carry it out. For I do not do the good I want to do, but the evil I do not want to do—this I keep on doing. Now if I do what I do not want to do, it is no longer I who do it, but it is sin living in me that does it.

So I find this law at work: Although I want to do good, evil is right there with me. For in my inner being I delight in God's law; but I see another law at work in me, waging war against the law of my mind and making me a prisoner of the law of sin at work within me. What a wretched man I am! Who will rescue me from this body that is subject to death? Thanks be to God, who delivers me through Jesus Christ our Lord!

So then, I myself in my mind am a slave to God's law, but in my sinful nature a slave to the law of sin. (ROMANS 7:14–25)

———

I'm the earnest, rich young ruler.[2]
I'm a prideful Pharisee.
I'm a Scribe obsessed with details,
High 'n' Mighty Sadducee.

I'm the skeptic . . . Doubting Thomas,[3]
Stubborn Pharaoh, . . . Jezebel.
I'm an arrogant Goliath,[4]
Often faring not so well.

I'm that angry Saul of Tarsus[5]
Who comes sometimes quite unglued . . .
Yes, a proud, cold-blooded killer
(Matthew five verse twenty-two'd).[6]

I'm like Sarah often laughing,[7]
And Elijah fleeing fast . . .
I'm like Peter in denial
When the rooster crowed at last.

I'm apostate way too often . . .
And a Gnostic know-it-all,
I'm a perfect Romans seven,
Son of Adam in free-Fall.

Like King David hearing Nathan,[8]
Like the darkness at the dawn . . .
I'm like Jonah sailing westward,[9]
Gomer going, going, . . . gone.[10]

I'm like Ahaz disobeying[11] . . .
And like Moses on the run.[12]
I'm a lukewarm good-for-nothing,
Like Isaiah, quite undone.[13]

———————

Who can help me? . . . Who can save me?
Who can turn this night to day?
Is there Someone who is able?
Good Lord, help me know The Way![14]

Father, God . . . Oh, Lord, have mercy!
Give us eyes to see our sin!
Help us mourn this grim condition;[15]
Help us look, Lord, deep within.

Help us gaze into that Mirror,
Of The Law's true Holy Light . . .
May we see true moral guilt there
And our existential plight.[16]

Plant the Seed of Truth within us;
Sow it deep, Lord, in the soul[17] . . .
Help us hear the Shepherd calling . . .
Help us turn into your Fold.

Help us see the Cross more clearly . . .
And His tortured, loving face,
Teach us daily why He came here:
Holy Love . . . Amazing Grace.

———————

There is therefore now no condemnation for those who are in Christ Jesus. For the law of the Spirit of life has set you free in Christ Jesus from the law of sin and death. For God has done what the law, weakened by the flesh, could not do. By sending his own Son in the likeness of sinful flesh and for sin, he condemned sin in the flesh, in order that the righteous requirement of the law might be fulfilled in us, who walk not according to the flesh but according to the Spirit. (ROMANS 8:1–4 ESV)

———————

Thank you, God, for such great mercy!
Thank you for the Victr'y won . . .
For the Blessed Hope[18] before us,
Promised King, returning Son.

WILL WE KNOW THE TRUTH IN TIME, SIR?

"Time itself is one more name for death."[1] —C. S. LEWIS

King Solomon, the human author of the book of Ecclesiastes, observed that our lives here "under the sun," our temporal enjoyments and pleasures, our loves, our accomplishments, our work, our gains and treasured acquisitions, will all be lost and forgotten—in the end all just meaningless vanities scattered like dust in the winds of time.

Matthew McCullough, in his book *Remember Death*, examines the fleeting impermanence of our lives on earth as the irreversible crush of time carries us along to that inevitable end. He writes: "Death spreads its poison through everything we enjoy because nothing we enjoy is ours to keep. Time passes, things change, and eventually everyone loses everything they love."[2]

———

Time's a deadly troublemaker . . .
Like an overwhelming wave.
Death is poison in the system . . .
And the situation's grave.

We've been told "Death's only natural . . ."
But it looks more like a curse.
Friend, the Juggernaut keeps rolling . . .
And the End can't be reversed.

Just in time, we have our season . . .
Then at last, the damning spell.
Just in time, is there Redemption?
Do you think, sir, time will tell?

Might the End be somehow thwarted?
Might this darkness flee at dawn?
Might we find there Revelation?
Might the Light of Truth come on?

Is this loss we all must suffer
Bound by time's futility?
Is there Someone with an answer?
Someone maybe with the Key?

Was there Someone who invaded,
Who like us was in the dock?
Is there Someone here with Good News?
Someone here who beat the clock?

Has decay, sir, been defeated?
Has that stone been rolled away?
Will we know the Truth in time, sir?
Will Grace have the final say?

Will we turn, turn, turn to seek Him?
Will He override our pride?
Will we bow in time before Him
Who for us was crucified?

Blessed be the God and Father of our Lord Jesus Christ!
According to his great mercy, he has caused us to be
born again to a living hope through the resurrection of

Jesus Christ from the dead, to an inheritance that is imperishable, undefiled, and unfading, kept in heaven for you, who by God's power are being guarded through faith for a salvation ready to be revealed in the last time. (1 PETER 1:3–5 ESV)

DID YOU WITNESS THE UNVEILING?

In the three synoptic Gospels (i.e., Matthew, Mark, and Luke), we are given an account of an apocalyptic[1] vision that has come to be known as "the transfiguration." Just prior to this dramatic "unveiling," Jesus had taken his disciples to Caesarea Phillipi, where the pagan worship of false (and lifeless) deities of nature was common and idolatrous sensual pleasures flourished. It was here that Jesus asked his disciples this simple question: "Who do *you* say I am?" And it was here that Peter responded: "You are the Christ, the Son of the living God."[2]

To confirm Peter's astonishing and radical conclusion, Jesus took Peter and two others (John and James) higher still upon a mountain:

> And after six days Jesus took with him Peter and James, and John his brother, and led them up a high mountain by themselves. And he was transfigured before them, and his face shone like the sun, and his clothes became white as light. And behold, there appeared to them Moses and Elijah, talking with him. And Peter said to Jesus, "Lord, it is good that we are here. If you wish, I will make three tents here, one for you and one for Moses and one for Elijah." He was still speaking when, behold, a bright cloud overshadowed them, and a voice from the cloud said, "This is my beloved Son, with whom I am well pleased; listen to him." When the disciples heard this, they fell on their faces and were terrified. But Jesus came and touched them, saying, "Rise, and have no fear." And when they lifted up their eyes, they saw no one but Jesus only.

And as they were coming down the mountain, Jesus commanded them, "Tell no one the vision, until the Son of Man is raised from the dead." (MATTHEW 17:1–9 ESV)

————

Were you with Him on the mountain?
Did you see Him, Peter, there?
Did you witness that unveiling . . .
Tremble in God's holy glare?

Did the Majesty astound you?
Did you fall, John, to your knees?
Did His Glory, James, engulf you
In the light of prophecies?

Did that bright Shekinah shock you?
Did you hear the Father's voice?
Did the bright cloud overwhelm you . . .
Then with tears did you rejoice?

Did Elijah stand before you?
And was Moses present, too?
God's two witnesses professing . . .
Future Blessed Hope in view.

Did God's grace then dawn upon you?
Did the Morning Star arise?
Did the Sun of Revelation
Manifest before your eyes?

Did the Word there overcome you?
Did it penetrate your soul?
Was the Seed of Truth implanted?
Did He add you to His fold?

Were your fears alleviated?
Were you changed forever there?
At long last, were you enabled
To escape the fowler's snare?

Were you born again that evening?
Were you rescued from the flood?
Did you wade into the true Light[3]—
Were you washed there by His blood?

———————

For we did not follow cleverly devised myths when we made known to you the power and coming of our Lord Jesus Christ, but we were eyewitnesses of his majesty. For when he received honor and glory from God the Father, and the voice was borne to him by the Majestic Glory, "This is my beloved Son, with whom I am well pleased," we ourselves heard this very voice borne from heaven, for we were with him on the holy mountain. And we have the prophetic word more fully confirmed, to which you will do well to pay attention as to a lamp shining in a dark place, until the day dawns and the morning star rises in your hearts, knowing this first of all, that no prophecy of Scripture comes from someone's own interpretation. For no prophecy was ever produced by the will of man, but men spoke from God as they were carried along by the Holy Spirit. (2 PETER 1:16–21 ESV)

THERE'S A BOMBSHELL IN THE CORNER

The Holy Bible was penned by numerous servants (prophets, apostles, and others) over the time-span of many centuries, even as it was conceived and authored in timeless Eternity by the One true God before being *breathed out* into time as one coherent and active Word. This, of course, is a profound mystery, but it is a mystery that continues to prove itself *explosively* true at each and every miraculous conversion. This fact is foolishness to those who are perishing, but to those who are being saved it is the good news of the power of God.[1]

––––––––––

"For the word of God is living and active, sharper than any two-edged sword, piercing to the division of soul and of spirit, of joints and of marrow, and discerning the thoughts and intentions of the heart." (HEBREWS 4:12 ESV)

"For I am not ashamed of the gospel, for it is the power of God for salvation to everyone who believes." (ROMANS 1:16 ESV)

––––––––––

There's a bombshell in the corner;
There's Good News from God Himself.
There's a message from Life's Author
There unopened on your shelf.

There's a skeptic deep within you,
One who lacks both faith and trust.
Does that stiff neck give you trouble
While the Scriptures gather dust?

Is that book you're passing over
Maybe something you should read?
Have the prophets and apostles
Shared a Word you ought to heed?

Is there Truth worth chewing over
In those pages left unread?
Living Water . . . Grace outpouring
At the Cross . . . Unleavened Bread?

Is true wisdom fast approaching
Bringing reverential fear?[2]
Might the Lamb of God be waiting?
Is the Bridegroom drawing near?

WHEN THIS TIME-BOUND BUBBLE'S OVER

Have you ever watched a small child chase a bubble as it floats by in the air? There is wonder and fascination in his eyes. The child is intrigued and mesmerized. And then, without warning, the bubble's delicate liquid membrane dissolves. The bubble bursts and disappears. Its time is up, and reality sets in. Our mortal lives on earth are like that, I think. Eventually, the delicate membrane of time dissolves. The things of the world, both the material and imagined things that we pursue, cherish, and desperately cling to will one day disappear. Those treasured baubles that mesmerize us and hold so much promise will simply vanish. All our temporal possessions, hopes, and dreams—all the idols of the flesh—will come to nothing in the end.

"For what will it profit a man if he gains the whole world and forfeits his soul? Or what shall a man give in return for his soul?" (MATTHEW 16:26 ESV)

Does this Time direct our passions?
Have we fallen for these "things"?
Do these baubles in this bubble
Rule us like despotic kings?

When life's vapor here does vanish,
What will Holiness reveal?
Will the sensate song of Satan
Keep us from the Truth that's real?

If the world, sir, has no windows,
Nothing left to see beyond,
Then the night will last forever . . .
Darkness with no hope of dawn.

Will this bubble burst to Glory,
Or will death and dark prevail?
Will the Son shine everlasting
When these mortal eyes have failed?

Is this matter all that matters?
Is the payoff worth it all?
Will these idols that we're hoarding
Be enough to break The Fall?

Will we search the Word of God, sir,
Or just proudly turn away?
Will we hear the Shepherd calling
Or remain the devil's prey?

Will the pride of life derail us?
Will the lust for power win?
Will eternal darkness find us
Bound by unforgiven sin?

Will the vein of silver purchase
The redemption we desire?
Will the weight of pride's possessions
Keep us from unending fire?

When this Time-bound bubble's over
When the final die is cast,
Will we know hell's outer darkness . . .
Or the Light of Truth at last?

Will the Blessed Hope embrace us?
Will we know the King has come?
Will the chains of death be broken?
Will the victory be won?

Will we be just fools forever?
Will delusion take its toll?
When this Time-bound bubble's over,
Will you forfeit, sir, your soul?

GOD'S RELENTLESS LOVE

God's true love is quite relentless;
If we would but turn around
Some will hear God's Mercy calling . . .
Some, it seems, won't hear a sound.

Some find blessing in submission,
Finding perfect Sabbath Rest.
Some will proudly keep on walking . . .
Truth forever unaddressed.

Will we dare turn back to listen?
Would we dare to count the cost?
Will the Shepherd/Bridegroom seek us?
Will we find Him at the cross?

———

On the whole, God's love for us is a much safer subject to think about than our love for Him. But the great
thing to remember is that, though our feelings come
and go, His love for us does not. It is not wearied by
our sins, or our indifference; and, therefore, it is quite
relentless in its determination that we shall be cured
of those sins, at whatever cost to us, at whatever cost
to Him.[1] —C. S. Lewis

AND LET COMFORT BE YOUR GUIDE

"While it lasts, the religion of worshipping oneself is the best. I have an elderly acquaintance of about eighty, who has lived a life of unbroken selfishness and self-admiration from the earliest years, and is, more or less, I regret to say, one of the happiest men I know. From the moral point of view it is very difficult! I am not approaching the question from that angle. As you perhaps know, I haven't always been a Christian. I didn't go to religion to make me happy. I always knew a bottle of Port would do that. If you want a religion to make you feel really comfortable, I certainly don't recommend Christianity.[1] —C. S. LEWIS

———

So the goal is what? Your comfort?
Being happy all day long?
If what's temporal is reigning,
Be my guest—just carry on.

If that bottle there is plenty,
Sir, to keep you satisfied,
Bottoms up! . . . (until it's empty),
And let Comfort be your guide.

If, however, there is Meaning . . .
If there's Truth outside these walls,
If the Shepherd's voice you're sensing,
I suggest you heed the call.

If just "happy" is your end game,
If there's that and Nothing more,
I pray someday you'll see writing
On the wall . . . and find the Door.

———————

"I am the door. If anyone enters by me, he will be saved and will go in and out and find pasture." (JOHN 10:9 ESV)

HAVE YOU WALKED HOME TO EMMAUS?

That very day two of them were going to a village named Emmaus, about seven miles from Jerusalem, and they were talking with each other about all these things that had happened. While they were talking and discussing together, Jesus himself drew near and went with them. But their eyes were kept from recognizing him. And he said to them, "What is this conversation that you are holding with each other as you walk?" And they stood still, looking sad. Then one of them, named Cleopas, answered him, "Are you the only visitor to Jerusalem who does not know the things that have happened there in these days?" And he said to them, "What things?" And they said to him, "Concerning Jesus of Nazareth, a man who was a prophet mighty in deed and word before God and all the people, and how our chief priests and rulers delivered him up to be condemned to death, and crucified him. But we had hoped that he was the one to redeem Israel. Yes, and besides all this, it is now the third day since these things happened. Moreover, some women of our company amazed us. They were at the tomb early in the morning, and when they did not find his body, they came back saying that they had even seen a vision of angels, who said that he was alive. Some of those who were with us went to the tomb and found it just as the women had said, but him they did not see. And he said to them, "O foolish ones, and slow of heart to believe all that the prophets have spoken! Was it not necessary that the Christ should suffer these things and enter into his glory?" And beginning with Moses and all the Prophets, he interpreted to them in all the Scriptures the things concerning himself. (LUKE 24:13–27 ESV)

When Jesus comes alongside, the Word comes alive, the shadows of obscurity recede, the spirit is quickened, the heart is stirred, Truth is revealed, and the darkness is chased by the dawn. The walk to Emmaus is like that . . .

Hello, Cleopas, how are you?
Why the long face? . . . Why the frown?
On this short walk to Emmaus,
Why on earth are you so down?

Let me show you what you're missing.
Let me open up your eyes!
Take a closer look at Scripture . . .
Moses right through Malachi.

All the scrolls were breathed about me
Just the Way the Father planned.
Don't be downcast . . . Search the Prophets.
Let me help you understand.

I'm the Author of the story . . .
I'm the Lamb who bled for you.
I'm the One who came to suffer.
I'm the Word who's now in view.

I'm the One Isaiah spoke of . . .
Crushed for man's iniquity.
I'm the greater Son of David
Come to set the prisoners free.

"It is written" . . . Moses saw me
(When I crushed the serpent's head).
I'm the ram caught in the thicket,
Mercy's Seat . . . Unleavened Bread.

I'm the Rock struck in the desert
From which Living Waters flowed.
I'm the Manna straight from heaven . . .
In the wilderness bestowed.

I'm the offering accepted . . .
Blood of Abel's sacrifice,
I'm the Shepherd David spoke of . . .
Israel's Redemption Price.

I'm the Ark, I'm Jacob's Ladder.
I'm the Tree of Life, my friend.
I'm the Way, sweet Land of Canaan,
The Beginning . . . and the End.

I'm the One the bulls surrounded,
I'm the One pierced on the tree,
I'm your Kinsman . . . your Redeemer . . .
I'm your Year of Jubilee!

———————

Cleopas,[1] proclaim the Good News . . .
Tell the world what you now know!
Share the Hope who dwells within you.
Sow the seed that it may grow.

JUST IN TIME

"If time is a brush which God paints on the canvas of the human heart, then Eternity is the perspective from which we get a look at the full perspective."[1] —RAVI ZACHARIAS

———————

"Just in time!" the lens we see through.
"Just in time!" now sets the stage.
"Just in time!" is why we scurry . . .
"Just in time!" our hourly wage.

"Just in time!" . . . a partial painting . . .
"Just in time!" portrays our plight.
"Just in time!" . . . both tempts and taunts us . . .
It's a snare that holds us tight.

"Just in time!" defines our meaning.
"Just in time!" then disappears.
"Just in time!" holds out its promise
But then always ends with tears.

———————

"Just in time!" gives false perspective . . .
But who's got the time to see?
Will we seek the Truth who's timeless,
Dwelling in Eternity?

———————

"He has also set eternity in the human heart; yet no one can fathom what God has done from beginning to end." (ECCLESIASTES 3:11)

BEAUTY NOT YET FATHOMED

In the Christian classic *The Weight of Glory,* C. S. Lewis elaborates on the true nature of beauty and the subtle nature of idolatry. The echoes of God's very existence, his beauty, his creativity, his power, and his glory press in upon us from every side through all the senses. We cannot *not* know that God exists. We are, the apostle Paul reminds us in the first chapter of the book of Romans, "without excuse"[1] in that regard. But at the same time, Lewis warns us to beware of the persistent danger of making an idol of those "things" that we may recognize as good.[2] We must look beyond and through the temporal . . .

Says Lewis,

> The books or the music in which we thought the beauty was located will betray us if we trust to them; it was not in them, it only came through them, and what came through them was longing. These things—the beauty, the memory of our own past—are good images of what we really desire; but if they are mistaken for the thing itself they turn into dumb idols, breaking the hearts of their worshipers. For they are not the thing itself; they are only the scent of a flower we have not found, the echo of a tune we have not heard, news from a country we have never yet visited.[3]

———

There's a Presence on this shoreline,
Precious scent for now that fails . . .
There's an Author . . . and we know it,
One who waits behind the veil.

By still water in reflection
There's a tug, a quiet pull,
There's a peace poured out by Grace there ...
There's a cup, though not yet full.

We may know reflected beauty,
But *true* Beauty lies beyond.
It's the Truth for which we're longing
As the darkness yearns for dawn.

There's a Beauty not yet fathomed ...
In a song not fully heard ...
A reminder of the longing
For a Love somehow deferred.

—————

May we see, Lord, through this beauty
To the Treasure greater still.
Give us grace to know our blindness
So that we may know Thy will.

—————

One thing I have asked from the LORD, that I shall seek:
That I may dwell in the house of the LORD all the days
    of my life,
To behold the beauty of the LORD
And to meditate in His temple. (PSALM 27:4 NASB)

IF YOU'RE THIRSTY

Once you were a child. Once you knew what inquiry was for. There was a time when you asked questions because you wanted answers, and were glad when you had found them. Become that child again. . . . You have gone far wrong. Thirst was made for water, inquiry was made for truth.[1] —C. S. Lewis

---

"But Jesus said, 'Let the little children come to me and do not hinder them, for to such belongs the kingdom of heaven.'" (Matthew 19:14 ESV)

If you're thirsty, find the water.
Break the devil's evil spell.
Seek the truth, and be rewarded.
Join the woman at the well.

Find the answer while He's calling.
Turn around, and you may see.
Taste the gospel's Living Water.[2]
Thirst no more eternally.

Find the One who came to find you.
Listen for the Shepherd's voice.
Come to Him as little children.
Bow before Him and rejoice!

ONLY JESUS KNEW THE SCORE

> Now as they were eating, Jesus took bread, and after blessing it broke it and gave it to the disciples, and said, "Take, eat; this is my body." And he took a cup, and when he had given thanks he gave it to them, saying, "Drink of it, all of you, for this is my blood of the covenant, which is poured out for many for the forgiveness of sins. I tell you I will not drink again of this fruit of the vine until that day when I drink it new with you in my Father's kingdom."
>
> And when they had sung a hymn, they went out to the Mount of Olives. (MATTHEW 26:26–30 ESV)

Scholars today can tell us with great assurance what hymn was sung that evening in the upper room at the conclusion of this final Passover fellowship meal commonly referred to as the "The Last Supper." The experts tell us that the disciples and the Lord would have sung the Hallel, as was the customary Jewish Passover tradition. Accordingly, the last hymn they would have sung would have been Psalm 118.

As Jesus sat with his disciples, He alone knew that within a few short hours He would be surrounded by an angry mob demanding His death. He knew what lay before Him. He knew that He would become God's true sacrificial Lamb. He knew that He would become the true Unleavened Bread to be broken. He knew He would be tortured and killed on a Roman cross, and He knew His blood would be poured out. And in the unfathomable wisdom of God, the Jewish Passover Hallel psalms written a thousand years earlier would prophetically dictate the script for Jesus and His disciples at this last communion supper.

Within just a few hours, two thousand years of prophetic shadow would "kiss" the Truth that had cast it. The pivot point of all history was about to occur. The words of Israel's prophets concerning Messiah were about to be fulfilled. And that evening . . . in the upper room . . . Jesus alone knew it.

Before leaving Jerusalem to go to the Mount of Olives and the Garden of Gethsemane, Jesus the Christ, Israel's long-promised Prophet, Priest, and King, surrounded for the last time by his disciples, lifted his voice, . . . with gladness and rejoicing . . . and sang about this long prophesied event and about "this day" that at sunset had just begun to unfold:

> Open to me the gates of righteousness,
>> that I may enter through them
>> and give thanks to the LORD.
> This is the gate of the LORD;
>> the righteous shall enter through it.
> I thank you that you have answered me
>> and have become my salvation.
> The stone that the builders rejected
>> has become the cornerstone.
> This is the LORD'S doing;
>> it is marvelous in our eyes.
> This is the day that the LORD has made;
>> let us rejoice and be glad in it.
>> (PSALM 118:19–24 ESV)

Jesus knew. The time had come. This was . . . at last . . . the Day!

And so they sang . . .
"This is the day that the LORD has made;
let us rejoice and be glad in it!"[1]

His disciples knew the words, of course, but only Jesus knew the score.

———————

When they sang the Hymn that evening,
Only Jesus knew the score . . .
Yes, those glad and joyful verses
Hid the pain that was in store.

Jesus saw the torture coming . . .
Crown of thorns pressed on his head,
Bloody scourging, cruel mocking,
Even as He broke the Bread.

Yes, He saw the Cross and soldiers;
He knew all the painful signs
That the Prophets once had spoken
Even as He poured the wine

He knew well there at the Table
Of the wicked heart of man . . .
He saw clearly Calv'ry's bloodshed,
Saw the nails go through His hands.

He saw spit and blood and anger . . .
And He saw his punctured side;
He knew death by crucifixion
Was the way He had to die.

Yes, the Stone to be rejected
Saw the writing on the wall.
He knew soon that He would suffer . . .
To obey the Father's Call.

But Christ saw beyond the torture,
Past the insult and the pain . . .
Past the taunts and past the jeering . . . ,
Wicked hearts of men insane.

So He sang this Hymn with gladness . . .
Soon the ransom would be paid!
God's Unleavened Bread provided . . .
On this day the Lord had made!

Yes, the Covenant long promised . . .
Hope of Blessing long foretold . . .
Would be "cut" in bloody crimson,
Now, at last . . . , it would unfold!

And so Death would now Pass over
Those whose Faith lies in the Lamb.
Ancient Promise made to Abram
Would destroy the Devil's scam.

See the Gate to Life and Glory
Swinging open now for all . . .
That through Faith His own might enter
God the Father's banquet hall.

Christ knew death could never keep Him . . .
Though He knew it lay ahead.
Resurrection frees the captives;
Taste this Wine and Broken Bread.

Friend, please come now to His Table
On this Day the Lord has made!
Sing Hosannah in the highest!
For the debt we owe . . . , He paid!

MAY WE HONOR YOU WITH WORSHIP

"Worthy are you, our Lord and God, to receive glory and honor and power, for you created all things, and by your will they existed and were created." (REVELATION 4:11 ESV)

The worshipping Christian must remember that God is an objective reality, not a subjective mental state. God exists independently of anyone's imagination, and to worship him necessarily requires that one turns one's attention away from contemplation of his own subjective experience and toward the God who is objectively "there."[1]—REBECCA MERRILL GROOTHUIS

"Worship is the proper response of all moral, sentient beings to God, ascribing all honor and worth to their Creator-God precisely because he is worthy, delightfully so."[2] —D. A. CARSON

Give us grace, Lord, to remember
When the Truth at last we heard,
When we trembled in your Presence
And our hearts at first were stirred.

You alone, dear God, are worthy;
Every blessing is from You.
By your will all things created
Will be recreated new.

You made all things for your Glory . . .
How unsearchable your ways!
May your Holy Spirit teach us . . .
You alone deserve our praise!

May we lift You up sincerely
By the things we say and do,
Find delight, Lord, in your splendor;
Draw us closer still to You.

Help us *know*, not just imagine
What You're doing . . . what You've done!
Bowing low in adoration
With thanksgiving for the Son.

May we honor You with worship
Magnify your Majesty.
Draw us to the Resurrection
Through the Cross of Calvary.

May your attributes of Beauty
Leave us speechless and in awe,
Help us lose ourselves in wonder
And your Holy Name applaud!

May we know Resurrection
May we know You here and now
May we honor and exalt You
In our hearts before you bow.

———————

"Ascribe to the LORD the glory due his name; worship the LORD in the splendor of his holiness." (PSALM 29:2)

"Come, let us bow down in worship, let us kneel before the LORD our Maker; for he is our God and we are the people of his pasture, the flock under his care." (PSALM 95:6–9)

THIS IS THE WAY—WALK IN IT

For a people shall dwell in Zion, in Jerusalem; you shall weep no more. He will surely be gracious to you at the sound of your cry. As soon as he hears it, he answers you. And though the LORD give you the bread of adversity and the water of affliction, yet your Teacher will not hide himself anymore, but your eyes shall see your Teacher. And your ears shall hear a word behind you, saying, "This is the way, walk in it," when you turn to the right or when you turn to the left. (ISAIAH 30:19–21 ESV)

When the waters of affliction
Grip us in the undertow . . .
When the mourning overwhelms us,
He's the One to whom we go.

When the wilderness surrounds us,
When we're fed the bread of pain,
Follow closely . . . these are lessons
From the Teacher-God who reigns.

When the desert jackals circle,
When the arrows start to fly,
Look to Jesus at Golgotha.
King of Glory, crucified.

He's the One who lifts our darkness,
And the Lamp unto our feet . . .
Guiding us into forever
Where our joy will be complete.

When we wander, He stays with us,
When we stumble, He is there.
He removes ungodly burdens
In this kingdom of the air.

Here's the Truth we should be trusting,
And the Life that never ends.
Here's the Way, now walk ye in it . . .
Perfect Grace the Father sends.

He will teach us, He will help us
As He guides both heart and soul.
When we stray away, He keeps us
On the path to streets of gold.

When that voice behind us whispers,
May we trust Him left or right.
In the midst of tribulation,
May we live by faith, not sight.

By His Power, for His Glory,
He gave all creation breath.
There's no longer need for weeping
Since He overpowered death.

———————

"Your word is a lamp to my feet and a light to my path."
(PSALM 119:105 ESV)

"He renews my strength. He guides me along right paths, bringing honor to his name." (Psalm 23:3 NLT)

"The Lord says, 'I will guide you along the best pathway for your life. I will advise you and watch over you.'" (Psalm 32:8 NLT)

"So I say, let the Holy Spirit guide your lives." (Galatians 5:16 NLT)

THE LORD MY SHEPHERD

The LORD is my shepherd; I shall not want.
    He maketh me to lie down in green pastures:
he leadeth me beside the still waters.
    He restoreth my soul: he leadeth me in the paths
of righteousness for his name's sake. (PSALM 23:1–3 KJV)

————

Is the Shepherd dwelling in you?
Is He guiding you along?
Is He coaxing you to follow . . .
Leading you away from wrong?

Do you trust Him in the darkness?
Does He cause you to rejoice?
Do you find His Grace sufficient
When you cannot hear His voice?

In the midst of tribulation
Do you find His Peace within?
Does His Promise of Forever
Make you long to live with Him?

Will your faith in Him sustain you
When this dark world lets you down?
Is the true Light shining through you?
Do you stand on Solid Ground?

If the Oil of Gladness keeps you,
You will never lose your Way.
When the Lamp of Truth is burning,
Even nighttime turns to day.

When the Word of revelation
Makes the strait way crystal clear,
Rest assured, the Son will guide you
To the Father drawing near.

He will comfort you in trouble;
He'll be there through every test,
Keep and bless you through each trial
And provide Eternal Rest.

He will never ever leave you.
He'll stand by you as a Friend,
He will walk with you forever,
And His love will never end.

———

"Be strong and courageous. Do not be afraid or terrified . . . for the LORD your God goes with you; he will never leave you nor forsake you." (DEUTERONOMY 31:6)

For I am convinced that neither death nor life, neither angels nor demons, neither the present nor the future, nor any powers, neither height nor depth, nor anything else in all creation, will be able to separate us from the love of God that is in Christ Jesus our Lord. (ROMANS 8:38–39)

ADORATION, LOST IN WONDER

In 1743 Charles Wesley penned these words, which later became
part of the beloved hymn titled "Love Divine, All Loves Excelling":

> Finish, then, Thy new creation
> Pure and spotless let us be;
> Let us see Thy great salvation
> Perfectly restored in Thee;
> Changed from glory unto glory
> Till with Thee we take our place,
> Till we cast our crowns before Thee,
> Lost in wonder, love and praise.[1]

———

> We will see God's boundless Glory,
> (Death will only see defeat).
> Life Eternal will embrace us,
> And our joy will be complete.
>
> Yes, the Fall will turn to Springtime
> When creation groans no more.
> We will see the Son in glory . . .
> And behold the distant shore.
>
> Yes, at last we'll know true freedom
> And we'll come to understand
> When we soar on wings of eagles,
> In God's *true* No Border Land.

Endless vistas will surround us,
Light sublime, revealing Grace . . .
Adoration, lost in wonder,
Gazing at the Savior's face.

In the end, there's only worship
That will never ever cease . . .
Then we'll know Eternal Beauty.
Then we'll see the Prince of Peace.

We will worship Him in wonder,
We will bow before the King.
We will praise Him for his Mercy,
And with all his angels sing.

———————

"The LORD reigns, let the earth be glad;
    let the distant shores rejoice. . . .
The mountains melt like wax before the LORD,
    before the Lord of all the earth.
The heavens proclaim his righteousness,
    and all peoples see his glory. . . .

Light shines on the righteous
    and joy on the upright in heart.
Rejoice in the Lord, you who are righteous,
    and praise his holy name." (PSALM 97:1, 5, 6, 11, 12)

ACKNOWLEDGMENTS

When I think about how *No Border Land* was conceived and how it developed over the years, I realize how grateful I am to so many . . . and for so many different reasons. There are simply too many people to thank here individually. But in that regard, I must acknowledge those Harris County, Georgia, friends (and family) who came alongside in the past with support, wisdom, spiritual guidance, and godly advice. You know who you are.

And more recently, I am truly indebted to pastors, Bible teachers, friends, and my now *extended* family in the Atlanta area (and beyond) who have directly and positively impacted my life and spiritual growth. Also, I would be remiss if I did not mention those innumerable encouragers, supporters, Christian scholars and apologists whom I have met online and from whom I have learned so much over the years. I thank you all.

But most of all, I want to thank my wife, Jane, for her faith in God and her selfless commitment to this project. This book would never have seen the light of day without her motivating influence. I would never have dreamed of publishing at all were it not for her vision and support. She was the midwife for *No Border Land* from beginning to end, pure and simple. She worked tirelessly to get the manuscript ready and presentable for publication. Her organizational expertise, her editorial skills, her eye for detail, and her wise advice were indispensible. She brought order out of chaos. God has graciously blessed me with such a helpmate, and I am forever grateful.

ENDNOTES

Introduction

1 Steve Turner, *Up To Date (Lion Publishing Corporation, 1982), pp. 138–139.*

2 Francis Schaeffer, A Christian View of Philosophy and Culture, Vol. 1, *The God Who Is There* (Crossway, 1994), p. 181.

3 Richard John Neuhaus, *Scandal Time Continued, "First Things: A Monthly Journal of Religion and Public Life," 2002, p. 81.*

4 Douglas Wilson, *A Serrated Edge* (Canon Press, 2003), p. 55.

5 Alexandr Solzhenitsyn, "Godlessness: The First Step to the Gulag," Templeton Prize lecture, London, May 10, 1983.

6 Carl F. Henry, *Twilight of a Great Civilization: The Drift Toward Neo-paganism* (Crossway, 1988), p. 27.

7 J. I. Packer, *"Fundamentalism" and the Word of God (Wm. B. Eerdmans Publishing, 1958), reprint, p. 168.*

Stir That New, Old Pagan Brew

1 William Shakespeare, "The Tragedy of Macbeth," Act 4, Scene 1.

2 Peter Kreeft, "Comparing Christianity & the New Paganism," http://www .peterkreeft.com/topics-more/religions_newpaganism.htm, (article reprinted from *Fundamentals of the Faith,* Ignatius Press, San Francisco, 1988).

Children of Chaos

1 Peter Atkins, *The Second Law* (New York: Scientific American, 1984), p. 200.

All Our Sacred Human Isms

1 Often attributed to G. K. Chesterton.

2 Phillip E. Johnson, *Reason in the Balance: The Case Against Naturalism in Science, Law, and Education* (Downers Grove, IL: InterVarsity Press, 1995), Introduction, p. 7.

Dr. Dumpty's Mass Dysfunction

1 Annette Kirk, joint talk with her husband, Russell Kirk, given at annual Seton-Neuman lecture at Catholic University, 1984; quote used by permission.

2 Lewis Carroll, *Through the Looking Glass* (MacMillan, 1871).

Come Jabberwock with Me Awhile

1 Alex Rosenberg, interview on website Rorotoko, "Cutting Edge Intellectual Interviews," November 6, 2011.

2 Alex Rosenberg, The *Atheist's Guide to Reality* (New York: W.W. Norton & Company, 2011), p. 239.

3 Ibid, pp.7–8.

4 *the vorpal sword*: Lewis Carroll said he could not explain this word, though it has been noted that it can be formed by taking letters alternately from "verbal" and "gospel."

5 Lewis Carroll, *Through the Looking Glass* (London: Macmillan, 1871), chapter 1.

6 Alex Rosenberg, ibid.

7 Thomas Howard, *Chance or the Dance?* 2nd Edition, "A Critique of Modern Secularism" (San Francisco: Ignatius Press, 2018), chapter 1, p. 1.

In the Meantime, Let Us Prey

1 Donna Gunderson Hailson, *The Rockery, Theology, Nature and the Arts as Spiritual Ambassadors for the Christian Faith*, e-magazine, August 7, 2016.

1984

1 George Orwell, *1984* (London: Secker & Warburg, 1949), p. 80.

Thank You So Much, Peter Pan

1 Hugh Hefner, *Los Angeles Times*, 1992.

2 Malcolm Muggeridge, www.orthodoxytoday.org/articles/MuggeridgeLiberal.php and @malmuggeridge .

3 Eric Hoffer, *Reflections on the Human Condition* (Hopewell Publications LLC, September 30, 2006).

Roe with Us into the Quagmire

1 Peter Kreeft, "A Baptism of the Imagination: A Conversation with Peter Kreeft," interview with Ellen Haroutunian, *Mars Hill Review* 5, Summer 1996, pp. 56–73.

2 Michael Novak, "Awakening from Nihilism: The Templeton Prize Address," *First Things*, August 1, 1994.

It's an Ivory-Towered Coup

1 George Orwell, essay "In Front of Your Nose," first published in Tribune, London, March 22, 1946.

Breathing in Those Noxious Fumes

1 Interview with Ken Campbell on *Reality on the Rocks: Beyond Our Ken* (1995).

2 Bertrand Russell, *Autobiography*, vol. 2 (London: George Allen and Unwin, 1968), p. 159.

3 Peter Singer, "The Sanctity of Life," *Foreign Policy*, September/October 2005 (as quoted in Utilitarian Philosophers website).

4 "Justifying Non-Christian Objections," a debate between Douglas Wilson and Farrell Till (transcript originally appeared in *Credenda/Agenda* [Vol. 7; No. 1]).

It's Why Klebold Pulled the Trigger

1 Michael Ruse, "Evolutionary Theory and Christian Ethics," in *The Darwinian Paradigm* (London: Routledge, 1989), pp. 262–269.

We Were There to Reclaim Eden

1 David Gates, "Twenty-Five Years Later, We're Still Living in Woodstock Nation" Cover Story, *Newsweek* 124.6 (1994).

2 1 Timothy 4:2.

3 John 3:16.

Bowing Low to Our Libido

1 Widely attributed to Mother Teresa, as on http://www.scmidnightflyer .com/mt.html, but some disagreement exists: https://en.wikiquote.org/wiki/ Talk:Mother_Teresa .

2 Ravi Zacharias, *Cries of the Heart* (Nashville, TN: Thomas Nelson, 2002), pp. 100–101.

Are the Consequences Clear Yet?

1 Robert P. George, social media post, then personal communication, used by permission, October 11, 2019.

2 "In the fourth generation your descendants will come back here, for the sin of the Amorites has not yet reached its full measure" (Genesis 15:16).

3 "Jesus said to him, 'I am the way, and the truth, and the life. No one comes to the Father except through me. If you had known me, you would have known my Father also. From now on you do know him and have seen him'" (John 14:6–7 ESV).

Followers of Fashion

1 Joseph Pearce, "The Eternal Shakespeare," *The Imaginative Conservative*, April 2014.

There's a Gould-ish Nightmare Brewing

1 Dr. Mark McMenamin, quote from the back cover of *Darwin's Doubt* by Stephen C. Meyer (New York: HarperCollins, 2013).

2 Dr. Russell Carlson, quote from the back cover of *Darwin's Doubt* by Stephen C. Meyer (New York: HarperCollins, 2013).

3 Lynn Margulis and Dorion Sagan, *Acquiring Genomes: A Theory of the Origins of the Species* (Basic Books, 2003), p. 29.

Where the Hatter Just Gets Madder

1 Friederich Nietzsche, *The Gay Science* (*Die fröhliche Wissenschaft*), section 125, "The Parable of the Madman," 1882.

2 Carl R. Trueman, *First Things*, "When You Detach the Earth From the Sun," December 2015 (http://www.firstthings.com/blogs/firstthoughts/2015/12/when -you-detach-the-earth-from-the-sun).

3 Ibid.

4 Hebrews 6:17–20.

Teaching Kids to Pick Their Gnosis

1 Widely attributed to George Orwell, as on https://www.azquotes.com/quote/ 445662 , but some disagreement: http://en.wikiquote.org/wiki/George_Orwell .

2 G. K. Chesterton, The Collected Works of G. K. Chesterton: Volume XXXIII, *The Defense of the Unconventional* (10-17-25): *The Illustrated London News: 1923–1925* (edited by Lawrence J. Clipper; general editors: George J. Marlin, Richard P. Rabatin, and John L. Swan [San Francisco: Ignatius Press, 1990]).

3 Yascha Mounk, "What an Audacious Hoax Reveals About Academia," *The Atlantic*, October 5, 2018, https://www.theatlantic.com/ideas/archive/2018/10/ new-sokal-hoax/572212/ .

4 Also referred to as the Sokal Affair: https://en.wikipedia.org/wiki/Sokal_affair— .

The Hemingway Is Here to Stay

1 Blaise Pascal, *Penseés, (43/199)* (Charleston, SC: BiblioLife, 2008), Penseés #434, 1670.

2 Peter Kreeft, *Love Is Stronger than Death* (San Francisco: Ignatius Press, 1992), chapter 1.

3 Ernest Hemingway, *For Whom the Bell Tolls* (New York: Scribner, 1995), first published October 1940.

4 Ernest Hemingway, *Death in the Afternoon* (New York: Vintage, 2000), first published in 1932.

Close Your Eyes and Make It Happen

1 Justice Anthony Kennedy, U.S. Supreme Court decision, *Planned Parenthood of Southeastern Pa. v. Casey*, 505 U. S. 833, 851 (1992).

2 "For God doth know that in the day ye eat thereof, then your eyes shall be opened, and ye shall be as gods . . ." (Genesis 3:5 KJV).

The Galapagos Sting

1 Phillip E. Johnson, JD, "How to Sink a Battleship: A call to separate materialist philosophy from empirical science," OrthodoxyToday.org, http://www .orthodoxytoday.org/articles/JohnsonBattleship.php .

Hawking Our Escape Plan

1 John Gray, "Alain de Botton's Atheist Temple Is a Nice Idea But a Defunct One," *The UK Guardian* (Opinion section), February 2012.

2 Genesis 3:4.

3 Genesis 3: 8 and John 3:19.

4 Genesis 2:16–17 and Exodus 20:3.

There's a Pile-Up on the Broad Way

1 C. S. Lewis, The Complete C. S. Lewis Signature Classics, Collected Letters of C. S. Lewis Series, *The Abolition of Man* (Grand Rapids, MI: Zondervan, 2002), p. 473.

2 "What sorrow awaits you teachers of religious law and you Pharisees. Hypocrites! For you are like whitewashed tombs—beautiful on the outside but filled on the inside with dead people's bones and all sorts of impurity" (Matthew 23:27 NLT).

3 Ravi Zacharias, "A Huge Blunder" (RZIM podcast), "Just a Thought" podcast, August 16, 2019, https://www.rzim.org/listen/just-a-thought/a-huge-blunder -1?fbclid=IwAR2M3bmNcMQVNWXSERZP0lyW-tYphjKutxhE9B3gCbJuezpq2rd es5tIR2s .

We Have Faith in Nothing Really!

1 The "Flying Spaghetti Monster" was first described in a satirical open letter written by Bobby Henderson in 2005 to protest the Kansas State Board of Education's decision to permit teaching intelligent design as an alternative to evolution in public school science classes (from Wikipedia).

2 Thomas Aquinas, *Summa Theologica* Part 1, Question 2, Article 3, from the Project Gutenberg eBook edition of *Summa Theologica*, translated by Fathers of the English Dominican Province.

3 Richard Rogers, "Something Good" (lyrics) from *The Sound of Music*, published 1965.

Peer into This Well, Whatever

1 John Milton, *Paradise Lost*, 1667.

All Those Tiny Lives in Newtown

1 Barack Obama, interfaith prayer vigil address, Newtown, Connecticut, October 16, 2012.

Mr. Nietzsche Saw It Coming

1 Friedrich Nietzsche, Walter Kaufmann's translation, appearing in *The Portable Nietzsche*, 1976 edition. Viking Press, pp. 6–47.

2 Hosea 8:7.

3 Matthew 7:24–7.

4 John 18:38.

5 Genesis 3:1.

6 Hebrews 4:12.

Dr. Singer May Be Singing

1 Molech is the name of the Canaanite god associated in the Old Testament with child sacrifice (see, e.g., Leviticus 18:21; 20:2–5).

2 King Crimson, album *In the Court of the Crimson King* (Epitaph, 1969).

3 "After ruling our thoughts and our decisions about life and death for nearly two thousand years, the traditional Western ethic has collapsed."6 Peter Singer, *Rethinking Life and Death: The Collapse of Our Traditional Ethics* (Melbourne, Australia: The Text Publishing Company, 1994), referenced in http://press-files .anu.edu.au/downloads/press/p82851/pdf/review_article02.pdf.

4 Peter Singer, *Rethinking Life and Death* (St. Martins Press, 1996).

5 Peter Singer, Princeton University Symposium, 2010.

6 Alberto Giubilini and Francesca Minerva, "After-birth Abortion: why should the baby live?" *Journal of Medical Ethics*, Vol. 39, Issue 5.

7 Tom Gilson, "Thinking Christian" blog, January 24, 2012: https://www. thinkingchristian.net/posts/2012/01/says-the-madman-humanity-is-dead-and -we-are-its-murderers/ .

Multiverses to the Rescue!

1 Nancy Pearcey, *Total Truth: Liberating Christianity from Its Cultural Captivity* (Wheaton, IL: Crossway Books, 2005), introduction to Part Two, p. 154.

Here in Babel We Hear Profits

1 Owen Strachan, "The Cessation of Planned Parenthood," Patheos blogs, "Thought Life," August 21, 2015, https://www.patheos.com/blogs/thoughtlife/ 2015/08/the-cessation-of-planned-parenthood/ .

2 Priscilla Smith, Director and Senior Fellow at the Program for the Study of Reproductive Justice at Yale Law School, speaking before Congressional hearing titled "Planned Parenthood Exposed: Examining the Horrific Abortion Practices at the Nation's Largest Abortion Provider," September 9, 2015.

Techno-Slabs of Beef in Action

1 Jerry Coyne, "Why you really don't have free will," *USA Today* op.ed., 2012.

2 James Barham, *What Is Life?* Part II: "The Poverty of Darwinism," December 30, 2011, https://pos-darwinista.blogspot.com/2011/ .

Ode To Mr. Nye-Guy

1 Bill Nye, addressing 2010 American Humanist Association conference, San Jose, California, on June 5, 2010, at 5:08 in video: https://www.youtube.com/watch?v=S4dZWbFs8T0 .

That's the Best That We Can Do

1 Eric Metaxas, *Christian Post* Opinion, "Absurdity Reigns . . . for Now: The Dictatorship of Relativism," September 22, 2016, https://www.christianpost.com/news/absurdity-reigns-for-now-the-dictatorship-of-relativism-169899/ .

Drawn and Quartered by the Storm

1 Blaise Pascal, from *Pensées* (first published in 1670).

2 William Blake, "Mock On, Mock on, Voltaire, Rousseau" (1800–1810), referenced in *The Portable William Blake,* Alfred Kazin, editor, Penguin, 1977.

Above the Moral Fray

1 Greg Koukl, "Intolerant Tolerance," transcript from *Stand to Reason* radio show, 2003, republished in *Salvo* emagazine, 2008.

Tell Yourself Somehow It Matters

1 T. H. White, *The Once and Future King* (Penguin, 2011), chapter 14.

2 Albert Mohler, *The End of History: The Moral Necessity of Eschatology*, Albert Mohler website/ blog, June 9, 2008.

Have You Read the News Today? . . . Oh, Boy

1 G. K. Chesterton, *Come to Think of It*, chapter XIX, "On Euphemisms," 1930.

2 Jeremiah 7:32.

3 Widely attributed to Malcolm Muggeridge; used on Ravi Zacharias's Facebook post: https://www.facebook.com/ravizacharias/posts/10151913123346813 .

Cruise the Neo-Pagan Waters

1 C. H. Spurgeon, "The Best Strengthening Medicine," Sermon No. 2209, *The Complete Works of C. H. Spurgeon*, vol. 37 (Delmarva Publications, June 1, 2015).

2 Mark Hitchcock, Jeff Kinley, interview with Oprah Winfrey on her *Super Soul Sunday* program, quoted in *The Coming Apostasy: Exposing the Sabotage of Christianity from Within* (NavPress, 2017), p. 117.

Pilgrims of Postmodern Preaching

1 Douglas Groothuis, Kingdom of God (personal blog), "Why I Think American Civilization Is Crumbling," March 12, 2015, https://douglasgroothuis.com/tag/kingdom-of-god/ .

Faith in Faith Removes All Doubt

1 Elisabeth Elliott, *Secure in the Everlasting Arms,* (Grand Rapids, MI: Revell, 2001).

Lure 'Em in with Sweet Concoctions

1 Genesis 3:4–5.

2 Galatians 1:6–9.

Therapeutic Puppy Dogma

1 Kenda Creasy Dean, *Almost Christian: What the Faith of Our Teenagers Is Telling the American Church* (Oxford University Press, 2010), p. 30.

2 James D. Conley, "Ubi Amor, Ibi Oculus," *First Things* (web edition): https://www .firstthings.com/web-exclusives/2015/03/ubi-amor-ibi-oculus, March 15, 2015.

Make a Wish for Heaven's Sake

1 J. C. Ryle, *Practical Religion* (Lulu. Com., publisher, 2018), pp. 532–533.

We Sing Hymns and Hers

1 Stuart McAllister, "Be Nice" (e-article), *A Slice of Infinity*, Ravi Zacharias International Ministry, 2012.

It's the Zeitgeist That We're Into

1 Friedrich Nietzsche, *The Gay Science*, para. 125, 1882, 1887, Walter Kaufmann, ed. (Vintage: New York, 1974), pp. 181–82.

2 G. K. Chesterton, *Everlasting Man* (Rough Draft Publishing, 2013).

Now The Gospel's Mostly Nice

1 A. W. Tozer, *The Quotable Tozer*, James L. Snyder, ed. (Grand Rapids, MI: Baker, 2018).

2 John MacArthur, *Ashamed of the Gospel*, 3rd edition (Crossway, 2001), p. 38.

Once We Even Used the Map

1 Douglas Groothuis, Facebook comment, August 5, 2019.

2 Sinclair Ferguson, "Apostasy and How It Happens," *Table Talk, April 2004.*

Flashes in the Pan

1 Martyn Lloyd-Jones, *Studies in the Sermon on the Mount* (Grand Rapids, MI: Wm. B. Eerdmans, reprint, 1976), p. 28.

2 Ibid, p. 5.

The God We're Now Divining

1 Ulrich Lehner, "No God But Santa," *First Things* (e-magazine), December 12, 2017.

He's the Robin Hood We Need!

1 John 8:44.

Faith in Pharaoh's Born Again

1 From the introduction of *Slouching Towards Gomorrah: Modern Liberalism and American Decline* by Robert H. Bork (New York: HarperCollins, 1996), in reference to the poem "The Second Coming," written by William Butler Yeats in 1919:

The darkness drops again; but now I know
That twenty centuries of stony sleep
Were vexed to nightmare by a rocking cradle,
And what rough beast, its hour come round at last,
Slouches towards Bethlehem to be born?

Care Bear God

1 Dorothy Sayers, *Creed or Chaos* (New York: Harcourt, Brace, 1949), pp. 5–6.

2 Gordon Clark, *In Defense of Theology* (Milford, MI: Mott Media, 1984), p. 119.

3 Gary L. Johnson, "Does Theology Still Matter?" in *The Coming Evangelical Crisis,* edited by John H. Armstrong (Chicago: Moody Press, 1996), pp. 65–67.

4 J. C. Ryle, *Holiness: Its Nature, Hindrances, and Roots* (Peabody, MA: Hendrickson Publishers, 2007), p. 224.

Preach It Laid-Back, Mellow, Lukewarm

1 A. W. Tozer, *The Radical Cross (Chicago: Moody Publishers, 2015).*

2 Ravi Zacharias, excerpt from video *The American Church,* 2010, found at https://rodiagnusdei.wordpress.com/2013/10/07/ravi-zacharias-on-the-american-church-the-problem-with-america-today-is-not-america-its-the-church/ .

Sifting through the Rubble

1 Greg Koukl, *Stand to Reason,* "20 Years of Clear-Thinking Christianity" (04/01/2013-18:13), https://www.str.org/articles/20-years-of-clear-thinking-christianity#.XWPtIOhKjIU .

2 Billy Graham, "Overcoming the Spirit of the Age," *Decision* Magazine, Billy Graham Evangelistic Association (published Oct. 6, 2017): https://www.billygraham.ca/stories/billy-graham-overcoming-the-spirit-of-the-age/ .

3 John Dewey (1859–1952) was an influential educational reformer and progressive in the late nineteenth to mid-twentieth centuries. He was a main proponent and originator of the philosophy of pragmatism and is often associated with the spread of situational ethics and moral relativism, in this way helping to prepare the way for the forces of postmodern deconstructionism so prevalent today in the early twenty-first century.

4 Mark 4:21–24.

Entertainment Sold as Worship

1 A. W. Tozer, *Keys to the Deeper Life,* revised edition (Clarion Classics, HarperCollins, 1988), p. 88.

2 James Montgomery Boice, *Whatever Happened to the Gospel of Grace? Rediscovering the Doctrines That Shook the World* (Crossway, 2009), chapter 3, p. 65.

Watch "the Fall" Now Fall from Favor

1 D. A. Carson, *Fallen: A Theology of Sin,* Christopher Morgan, Robert Peterson, eds. (Crossway, 2013), p. 22.

2 1 Peter 5:8–9.

3 Psalm 27:8–9.

4 Luke 14:28–30.

In the Lukewarm Water Doldrums

1 David Wells, *Losing Our Virtue* (Wm. B. Eerdman Publishing, 1999), p. 29.

2 C. S. Lewis, *Mere Christianity* (1952; reprint San Francisco: HarperSanFrancisco, 2001), p. 56.

3 "A quote by Malcolm Muggeridge." theysaidso.com, 2019: https://theysaidso.com/quote/malcolm-muggeridge-the-depravity-of-man-is-at-once-the-most-empirically-verifiab, accessed September 4, 2019.

Love Declares Just Condemnation

1 C. S. Lewis, *The Problem of Pain* (Simon & Shuster, 1996).

2 Michael Horton, *Christless Christianity: the Alternative Gospel of the American Church* (Grand Rapids, MI: Baker, 2008), p. 104.

Everybody's Chasing Happy

1 C. S. Lewis, from blog "Should Christianity Be Sold with A Warning Label?" On blogspot "The Wisdom of C. S. Lewis," July 27, 2011: https://cslewiswisdom.blogspot.com/2011/07/should-christianity-be-sold-with.html .

2 C. S. Lewis, *The Joyful Christian* (New York: Macmillan, 1977).

Lord, Reveal Our Destitution

1 David Wells, *Losing Our Virtue: Why the Church Must Recover Its Moral Vision* (Grand Rapids, MI: Wm. B. Eerdmans, 1999), p. 39.

2 Isaiah 30:19–21.

3 2 Samuel 12:5–7.

4 John 3:19–20.

5 Psalm 51:17.

6 Matthew 5:4.

7 Luke 15:22–24.

8 Matthew 5:3–6.

9 Ibid.

10 Ibid.

11 Isaiah 42:7.

12 John 3:18.

13 Ephesians 2:1–2.

14 Romans 5: 9–11.

15 Malachi 4:2.

16 John 14:6.

17 Luke 9:51.

18 Romans 3:10–18.

19 Isaiah 64:6.

20 Ephesians 1:13–14.

Did You Tip That Righteous Scale?

1 John M. Frame, *Apologetics: A Justification of Christian Belief* (Phillipsburg, NJ: P&R Publishing, 2015).

Maybe If We're Honest

1 Alexandr Solzhenitsyn, *The Gulag Archipelago 1918–1956* (New York: HarperCollins, 1979).

2 Peter Kreeft, *Handbook of Christian Apologetic* by Peter Kreeft and Ronald Tacelli (InterVarsity Press, 1994).

Simple Parables of Beauty

1 Steve De Witt, *Eyes Wide Open: Enjoying God in Everything* (Grand Rapids, MI: Credo House Publishers, 2012).

2 C. S. Lewis, *The Weight of Glory* (San Francisco: HarperOne, revised edition, 2001).

Someone, Quick! Go Find Josiah!

1 See Romans 2:12–16 for details.

2 James Montgomery Boice, *Foundations of the Christian Faith* (InterVarsity Press, revised edition, 2019) p. 223.

Yes, The Prophets Saw Him Coming

1 Genesis 3:15; 22:8–12.

2 Genesis 22:8–12.

3 Exodus 12:5–7; 1 Corinthians 5:7–8.

4 Genesis 15:6.

5 Genesis 45:1–7.

6 Genesis 45.

7 Psalm 110.

8 Malachi 4:1–6.

9 Ruth 4:9–11.

10 Daniel 9:25.

11 Micah 5:2.

12 Isaiah 53.

13 Isaiah 53:4.

14 Isaiah 55:1–2; Matthew 5:6.

15 Genesis 15:6.

16 Hebrews 8:5.

17 Numbers 12:3; Matthew 5:5.

18 Isaiah 66:1–2.

In Obscurity They Found Him

1 Marvin Rosenthal, "The Perfect Timing of the Coming of Christ," Zion's Hope (on-line), December 26, 2017, https://www.facebook.com/notes/zions-hope/the-perfect-timing-of-the-coming-of-christ/334968723652526/ .

2 "When the perishable has been clothed with the imperishable, and the mortal with immortality, then the saying that is written will come true: 'Death has been swallowed up in victory'" (1 Corinthians 15:54).

Hold Me Up to His Example

1 Matthew 5:3.

2 Matthew 5:6.

3 Romans 3:9–20.

4 2 Samuel 12:17.

5 Isaiah 64:6.

6 Matthew 7:13–14.

7 G. K. Chesterton, *Illustrated London News*, March 2, 1929.

Truth May Simply Say "I AM"

1 Donald Williams, "Where is the Battle?" January 11, 2016, http://thefivepilgrims
.com/2016/01/11/where-is-the-battle/.

He's the Justice Man Is Dreading

1 Peter Kreeft, "How to Save Western Civilization: C. S. Lewis as Prophet," chapter
1 of *C. S. Lewis for the Third Millenium: Six Essays on the Abolition of Man* (Ignatius
Press, 1994).

2 Matthew 5:4.

3 Matthew 5:3.

4 1 Peter 4:5.

5 Matthew 5:7.

6 Ravi Zacharias Quotes. BrainyQuote.com, BrainyMedia, Inc, 2019, https://www
.brainyquote.com/quotes/ravi_zacharias_527673, accessed November 7, 2019.

Furnace of Affliction

1 J. R. Miller, *When the Song Begins* (New York: Thomas Y. Crowell & Co., 1905),
chapter 2, "The Mystery of Suffering, pp. 22–23.

2 Eugene Nation, Sunday school lesson, Hickory Road Baptist Church, Canton, GA,
January 26, 2020, used by permission.

3 Job, chapter 11.

Lord, Put Down This Grim Rebellion

1 Matthew 16:5–12.

2 Matthew 7:13–14.

3 John 10:7.

4 Matthew 5:4.

5 Psalm 119:18.

6 Exodus 34:6–7.

7 Galatians 3:24.

8 1 John 5:1–5.

9 Proverbs 11:2.

10 Matthew 16:17.

11 Matthew 16:19.

12 Matthew 13:31.

13 Luke 4:18–19.

14 Matthew 16:18.

15 Revelation 19:7.

There's a Romance from the Start

1 Douglas Groothuis, "A Short Theology of Listening," Douglas Groothuis, PhD (blog), June 7, 2014.

Will We Dwell within His Tent?

1 "All the stars in the sky will be dissolved and the heavens rolled up like a scroll; all the starry host will fall like withered leaves from the vine, like shriveled figs from the fig tree" (Isaiah 34:4).

2 "For the grace of God has appeared, bringing salvation for all people, training us to renounce ungodliness and worldly passions, and to live self-controlled, upright, and godly lives in the present age, waiting for our blessed hope, the appearing of the glory of our great God and Savior Jesus Christ" (Titus 2:11–13 ESV).

I'm a Perfect Romans Seven

1 Cardinal Timothy Dolan, Presidential Address, USCCB Plenary in Baltimore, 2012.

2 Luke 18:23–25.

3 John 20:25.

4 1 Samuel 17:10.

5 Acts 9:1.

6 Matthew 5:22.

7 Genesis 18:12.

8 2 Samuel 12:5–7.

9 Jonah 1:1–3.

10 Hosea 4:12.

11 Isaiah 7:10–12.

12 Exodus 2:15.

13 Isaiah 6:5.

14 John 14:6.

15 Romans 3:9–18; Matthew 5:4.

16 John 3:18–19.

17 Matthew 13:18–23.

18 Titus 2:11–14.

Will We Know the Truth in Time, Sir?

1 C. S. Lewis, *A Grief Observed* (New York: HarperOne, 1963).

Did You Witness the Unveiling?

1 The primary meaning for the Greek word *apocalypsis* is "revelation," that is, an unveiling or unfolding of things not previously known and which could not be known apart from the unveiling.

2 See Matthew 16:13–17.

3 1 John 2:8.

There's a Bombshell in the Corner

1   See 1 Corinthians 1.

2   "The fear of the LORD is the beginning of wisdom, and knowledge of the Holy One is understanding" (Proverbs 9:10).

God's Relentless Love

1   C. S. Lewis, *Mere Christianity* (1952; HarperCollins: 2001), pp. 132–133.

And Let Comfort Be Your Guide

1   C. S. Lewis, *God in the Dock* (HarperCollins, revised edition, 2001).

Have You Walked Home to Emmaus?

1   Cleopas means "proclaimer" in the Greek.

Just In Time

1   Attributed to Ravi Zacharias, as on https://www.christianquotes.info/images/3-ways-gods-at-work-in-you/ .

Beauty Not Yet Fathomed

1   Romans 1:20.

2   1 John 5:21.

3   C. S. Lewis, *The Weight of Glory* (New York: Macmillan and Co., 1966), pp. 4–5.

If You're Thirsty

1   C. S. Lewis, *The Great Divorce* (New York: MacMillan Publishing Company, Inc., 1946).

2   John 7:38.

Only Jesus Knew the Score

1   Psalm 118:24

May We Honor You with Worship

1   Rebecca Merrill Groothuis, "Putting Worship in the Worship Service," in Douglas Groothuis, *Christianity That Counts: Being a Christian in a Non-Christian World* (Grand Rapids, MI: Baker, 1994), p. 76.

2   D. A. Carson, "Worship under the Word," in *Worship by the Book*, ed. D. A. Carson (Grand Rapids, MI: Zondervan, 2002), p. 26.

Adoration, Lost in Wonder

1   Charles Wesley, "Love Divine, All Love Excelling," 1743.